THE HISTORY

OF

MR. SEWARD'S PET

IN

EGYPT.

His Acts Denounced, and His Usurpations Condemned by the Courts.

MEMORIAL.

To the Honorable the Senate and House of Representatives of the United States of America:

The memorial of Francis Dainese, a citizen of the United States, residing at Washington, D. C., respectfully shows:

That on the 5th of September, 1863, while your memorialist was temporarily in Egypt, Mr. Thayer, then United States Consul General at Alexandria, having, on account of ill health, obtained leave of absence, solicited and appointed him to act in his stead until his return; that he presented him to His Highness the Viceroy as acting consul general and accredited him as such to the Egyptian authorities, to the foreign representatives, and to our captains of armed vessels and others, by official circulars and commission bearing date 5th September, 1863, at the same time giving notice thereof to the Department of State in his despatch No. 38 of same date. (See Appendix, pp. 1–4; Nos. 1 to 6.)

That many American claims against the Egyptian Government being then pending, Mr. Thayer, in presenting your memorialist to the Viceroy, demanded their early settlement, which His Highness promised to effect.

That in consequence of telegrams received from Mr. Adams, our Minister in London, and Mr. Dudley, our consul at Liverpool, to the effect that the two notorious Birkenhead iron-clad rams were being prepared for sea, apparently for the Viceroy's service, but in reality for the use of persons in armed rebellion against the United States Government, your memorialist, with a view to prevent their sailing and consequent prey upon our commerce, exerted himself in obtaining from the Egyptian Government an official denial of its alleged ownership of these rams, and forwarded the same

September 11, 1863, by telegraph, to Mr. Adams, apprising also of the fact the State Department, by his despatch No. 39; which proof reached London in time to baffle the only plea then made against their detention, namely, the plea that they belonged to the Viceroy of Egypt, and secured their long looked for seizure. That a later attempt to free them on other grounds was also defeated by additional proof, sent by your memorialist to our Ministers in Paris and London, and duly communicated to the State Department by his despatch, No. 41. (See Appendix, pp. 4–7, Nos. 7 to 11.)

That shortly thereafter, your memorialist settled, at no little labor, in our favor, a long mooted question of jurisdiction, which arose between the American and British consulates in Egypt, adjusting, upon principles of international law, the points involved, to the general approval of the government and people of Egypt, and to Mr. Thayer's particular satisfaction. (See despatches Nos. 40 and 42 to State Department, with accompanying papers in Appendix, pp. 8–16, Nos. 12–16, and Mr. Thayer's letter, p. 16, No. 17.)

That later it devolved upon your memorialist to conduct our vice-consulate at Cairo, at his own expense, (it being an unsalaried office,) and, at Mr. Thayer's especial request, to establish consular agencies and press the Viceroy to settle the claims of our protégés. (See Appendix, pp. 16–22, Nos. 18–24.

That Mr. Seward having extended indefinitely Mr. Thayer's leave of absence, he *did not return* to Egypt until December, 1863, and then, his health still being feeble, *he did not resume his office, nor did he make his return officially known* to the Egyptian government and the foreign representatives, but remained *incognito*, partly at Cairo, partly at Suez, and lastly in Alexandria, where he died. All that time your memorialist, under his credentials, transacted all the business of the consulate general, and kept up a laborious correspondence with the local government and the foreign representatives, but submitting all matters to Mr. Thayer, and conducting the same with his advice and consent. (See Appendix, pages 24–36, Nos. 25–37.)

That the Viceroy not having fulfilled his promise *to settle the pending American claims*, at Mr. Thayer's request, your memorialist, on the 9th of February, 1864, filed a protest against the Egyptian government, (see Appendix, page 29, No. 30,) which protest failing to produce the desired result, Mr. Thayer wrote him on the 24th of same month to proceed to Cairo for additional *siege operations*. (See Appendix, page 35, No. 35.) That he went thither, and after consultation with him, he, by his direction, intimated to the Egyptian minister for foreign affairs that a persistence in this denial of justice would compel us to strike our flag and suspend diplomatic relations, which intimation elicited excuses and a renewal of promises for a speedy settlement, pending which Mr. Thayer died, without ever having resumed his official position, and while your memorialist, under his credentials, was still the only recognized U. S. representative in Egypt; a circumstance which left the latter no alternative but to continue, as he did, in the charge entrusted to him by Mr. Thayer, and follow his policy until the State Department, duly informed by him of his death, (see Appendix, page 38, No. 50,) should send a new consul or give other instructions.

That the only notice Mr. Seward took of your memorialists' information was the appointing of a favorite with permission to travel four months to the European watering places, whence he arrived in Egypt August 17, 1864, and forthwith commenced perpetrating the iniquities hereinafter stated. This favorite was Charles Hale.

That while awaiting instructions from the State Department, your memorialist, in his official character, received and presented to the Viceroy the officers of the United States ship Constellation, attended the citizens, furnished relief to the widows and orphans of our soldiers, sent to the revenue officers the certificates required by law for the collection of revenue, kept the Department of State informed of the state of affairs at the consulate, and performed every other duty his official position required.

That on the 15th of July, 1864, the Egyptian police violated an American domicil—that of Mr. Kindineco—beat the owner, and maltreated and dragged his servants to prison. For these wrongs your memorialist demanded such reparation as international law and the custom in Egypt required.* This being declined, your memorialist, following the course of his colleagues, acted as they did in like cases, namely; he notified the Egyptian government that unless the demanded reparation be given within a stated time he would strike his flag and suspend diplomatic relations;† and as this was not timely complied with he struck his flag.‡ (See Appendix, page 48, No. 41.

This latter course had the desired effect of inducing the Viceroy to commission Mr. Tastu, consul general and diplomatic agent of France, to meet your memorialist and arrange the difficulty. Negotiations were at once commenced through that high-toned functionary, and a suitable reparation, with the settlement of the pending claims, had already been promised by the Viceroy. An arrangement mutually satisfactory and honorable was thus on the eve of being effected, when the reported insidious advice sent to the Viceroy by our own official, Mr. Brown,‖ then temporarily in

---

* The custom in the East, established by numerous precedents, for insults to the flag, or those under its protection, is to demand the dismissal and punishment of the offenders.

† In the spring of 1863 Mr. De Beauval, acting consul-general of France, demanded reparation for ill-treatment to a Frenchman; the Viceroy delayed complying with the demand. The acting consul intimated that unless immediately granted he should strike his flag. It was at once granted by the *dismissal*, *degradation* and *banishment* of the military officers and soldiers who were guilty of the offence. (See dispatch 54 in Appendix, page 48, No. 41.) In 1865 an Italian was insulted. Mr. Bruno, Italian consul-general, followed the same course and obtained *full* reparation. (See note in Appendix, page 84, No. 68.)

‡ In 1852 Mr McCauley, United States consul-general in Egypt, having demanded and being denied reparation for violation of domicil, he notified the Viceroy that unless it be given within a stated time he should strike his flag. The Viceroy delayed. Mr. McCauley struck his flag. The Viceroy then entered into negotiations, (exactly in the way as did the present Viceroy,) and granted the demanded reparation with indemnity. Mr. Webster *approved* the course pursued by Mr. McCauley.

‖ Mr. Brown, as already stated, advised the Viceroy that the manager of the consulate-general in Egypt, being without *exequator* from the Sultan, he might consider him as not officially recognized, and use that as a pretext to waive the demanded reparation.

This insidious advice had the double effect of preventing the consummation

charge of our legation at Constantinople, suspended its consummation, (see despatch No. 56 in Appendix, page No. 51,) and Mr. Hale's subsequent action completed our humiliation, sacrificed the interests of our protégés, and so dishonored our flag in Egypt that nothing but a significant rebuke of Congress can again restore it to its former standing.

Mr. Hale reached Alexandria the 17th of August, 1864. On his arrival your memorialist received him in his house as a guest, informed him of the state of affairs and of his course, *which he promised to sustain*, notified his colleagues of the new consul's arrival, made over to him the consular property, and withdrew from further connection with the office. A

---

of your memorialist's advantageous arrangement through Mr. Tastu, and of setting at defiance Mr. Seward's policy of direct intercourse with Egypt, as the sequel will explain.

By the convention of 1840, between England, Russia, Austria, and Prussia, the succession to the governorship of Egypt was secured to the lineal descent of Mohamed Ali, under the "suzereinty" of the Sultan of Turkey.

Since that time the successors of Mohamed Ali have received their investiture from the Sultan, and the representatives to the Viceroy from the powers of Europe have uniformly been accredited *to His Imperial Majesty the Sultan, to reside in Egypt*, and have received the Sultan's *exequator* to that effect through their respective legations at Constantinople, who thereby exercise a certain control over them.

Contrary to the above practice, Mr. Seward, in 1861, accredited W. S. Thayer, Esq., directly *to His Highness the Viceroy of Egypt*, and this dispensed with the necessity of obtaining an *exequator* from the Sultan, at the same time that it took away from our legation at Constantinople its presumptive control.

The Viceroy, considering a direct recognition from our Republic as amounting to his independence, corresponded directly with President Lincoln, and, during his reign, indulged in acts defiant to the Sultan's authority; among which the *raising, equipping, and furnishing an armed regiment of Arabs* to His Imperial Majesty Napoleon III, in 1862, to assist in establishing the Archduke Maximilian in Mexico.

Whether Mr. Seward's policy *in recognizing and establishing direct intercourse with the tributary of an ally*, and thereby inflating his desire to rebel against his master, especially at the peculiar epoch when we were struggling at home to keep the South in subjection, was a diplomatic *faux pas*, Mr. Brown was not called upon to decide. He was a subordinate, and in duty bound to adhere to his chief's policy; and as Mr. Thayer had already been directly *recognized* by the Viceroy as the accredited agent of this Government in Egypt, and, under his credentials and recognition, he accredited your memorialist, who was likewise *recognized*, and, like Mr. Thayer, acted pursuant to that policy, (see Appendix, pages 19, 22, and 24; Nos. 22, 24, and 25,) Mr. Brown had no business to interfere. Yet he intrigued and tried, during Mr. Thayer's lifetime, to bring him under the old rule; and, failing with Mr. Thayer, he seized the opportunity of the difficulty between Mr. Thayer's deputy and the Viceroy to open to the latter a path by which to dodge surrender; and Mr. Seward, regardless of consistency in enforcing his own policy—to say nothing of the trampled honor of our flag—permitted Mr. Brown's conduct to pass unrebuked!

few days thereafter, and after a dozen of secret interviews between said Hale and a Jew banker, a confidential agent of the Viceroy in pecuniary affairs, he changed tactics and again hoisted the consular flag *unavenged*, without any satisfaction for the violation of domicil and insult to the consular authority, or the settlement of the pending American claims, (see Appendix, page 64; No. 56,) though well founded public opinion accused him of having received in exchange from His Highness the Viceroy a present of twenty thousand pounds sterling, for which he was denounced in every public place in Egypt and through the newspapers, (see Appendix, pages 40, 71, 72, 76, and 83; Nos. 39, 60, 61, 63, and 66,) and was caricatured *as pulling up with one hand* the American flag by the weight of a bag of coin in his other hand!

Your memorialist devoted to our country his services in Egypt, to the best of his abilities, for about a year, without demanding or receiving any pay, nor has he even been reimbursed of his expenses for the support of the consulate from Mr. Thayer's death to Mr. Hale's arrival; and neither has he had an acknowledgment from this Government in return for these unpaid services; but instead thereof he has been unjustly persecuted, plundered, and otherwise improperly dealt with by Mr. Hale, as hereinafter explained; and having, after a persisted denial of justice by the Executive, applied to and obtained from our courts (see Appendix, pages 86–91; Nos. 70–75) all the legal remedy they could afford against an executive officer beyond their reach, and whose wrongful acts are sustained by his immediate chief, he now submits the case to the representatives of the nation for final legislative redress.

The official derelictions now submitted to the judgment of Congress, are of a twofold character, viz: first, those which involve national dignity, and which it is every citizen's duty to bring to public notice; and, secondly, those which wrought injury and ruin to your memorialist for which he solicits personal redress.

In the first category must be placed, first, Mr. Hale's official subserviency to the influences which induced him to rehoist unavenged the U. S. flag, and to abandon and sacrifice the American claims at a moment when his least exhibition of firmness or adherence to your memorialist's course would have satisfied the former and settled the latter ; secondly, his atrocious proceeding in withdrawing, October 30, 1863, (see Appendix, p. 46 ; No. 40,) from Thomas Kindineco and Joseph Santi, the protection of the American flag, to which they were justly entitled,* and placing them, their families and their interest, at the tender mercies of the Egyptian government, whose enmity to them Mr. Hale well knew, and who have been thereby totally ruined ; third, his bold step in the path of official falsehood in assuring the Egyptian government, *in the face of your memorialist's credentials*, on file in the archives of the Egyptian government, and the

---

*Kindineco was a merchant, and proceeded to Egypt from New York, in 1861 ; Santi was the editor of the newspaper "Popolo," published at Alexandria, and went there also from New York, in 1864.

Both landed under the cover of the American flag, were admitted by the consulate general to its protection, and were so recognized by the Egyptian government. When Mr. Hale withdrew American protection from them, the former fled for his life, the other was thrown in a dungeon, and his printing office was literally gutted by the local police, from whose hands his individual person was, for humanity's sake, finally rescued by the Italian Consul General. Santi's offence was the censuring of Hale's conduct in relinquishing American rights.

Hale and his protectors alleged in excuse of the abandonment of these persons, that they were not naturalized, but had only declared their intentions to become American citizens, and were not therefore entitled to protection abroad; this is a fallacy, and only shows that they restrict themselves within the narrow limits of the local laws which define and regulate the rights of citizens in the United States, instead of standing on the broad platform of international law by which we are governed abroad ; and although the former deny to those not yet naturalized the exercise of the citizen's full right in our own land, the latter clothe with equal protection all those travelling under a nation's flag in a foreign land, and particularly in the Mohammedan countries. Hence, by the terms of the capitulation of 1595, between Turkey and England, all persons being in the dominions of Turkey under English protection are to be deemed British subjects and respected accordingly ; and by that of 1604, between that power and France, those under French colors are to be considered and respected as Frenchmen. These capitulations form the basis of all subsequent treaties, and our treaties placing us on the footing of the most favored nations impose upon us the obligation to protect and defend those whom we have admitted under our protection. And this is fully illustrated in Mr. Marcy's firm attitude in the Cozsta case, (Wheaton's International law, 6th edition, page 128 and sequel.) As Kindineco and Santi went to Egypt under cover of the American flag, were admitted to its protection, and so recognized by the Egyptian government, and that they were subsequently insulted while under its protection, the shame of the insults offered them reflects upon our flag, not upon their individual persons, and all the reasons adduced to the contrary are mere subterfuges, set up to cover an inglorious deed, and are to this day held in contempt in Egypt by the very men who did the wrong and by all others—a fact which Congress can easily ascertain by sending there a delegate to investigate the matter.

foreign representatives, and of *Mr. Thayer's instructions* respecting the course to be pursued, that your memorialist had acted as Consul General *without authority, and that his course in defending the honor of our flag and in insisting upon the settlement of the claims entitled to its protection, was an affair to be regretted*, (see Appendix, pp. 46–47, No. 40,) and also in falsely asserting President Lincoln's authority for the committal of the atrocities against Kindineco and Santi, and for the denunciations against your memorialist, when the fact is that Mr. Lincoln knew nothing of the matter, and so assured your memorialist.

Passing from these public and proved betrayals of national principles to the individual wrongs, your memorialist must premise, that when Mr. Hale, yielding to temptation, repudiated the course of Mr. Thayer and your memorialist, the latter deemed it a duty to report the fact to our Government, which he did in a despatch, No. 57, addressed to the Secretary of State. (See Appendix, page 64, No. 56.)

Forgetful of the rules of hospitality and of his duty as a guest, Mr. Hale unceremoniously possessed himself of your memorialist's house with its contents, intercepted and opened his letters, broke open and plundered two locked rooms, and seized the money, books, effects, and private papers therein, among which was part of your memorialist's correspondence wherein his conduct was exposed, (see Appendix, pp. 67, 68, No. 57, 58;) and he did this while your memorialist was ill, crippled by rheumatism, and totally incapacitated of the use of arm and limb.

Your memorialist thereupon quitted Egypt for the mineral baths, to seek a relief from his disease, and thence proceeded home. In quitting Egypt he left in charge of his friends a large amount of American machinery, agricultural implements, &c., &c., which he was introducing there, and also many notes and claims for collection. While at the baths he received a copy of Mr. Hale's address to the Viceroy, hereinbefore alluded to. (See Appendix, page 46, No. 40.) This address, humiliating to the United States, and derogatory to your memorialist, having been delivered after sufficient time had elapsed to have brought a check from the

State Department upon Hale's conduct, reported in despatch No. 57, satisfied your memorialist that Mr. Seward's old enmity to him, and perhaps other private considerations, had prevailed over that functionary's duties as a public officer, and disposed him to overlook national honor and private rights. Wherefore your memorialist reported the whole affair to President Lincoln. (See Appendix, page 40, No. 39.) This report and accompanying papers were delivered to the President by a distinguished Senator here present; but the President, absorbed at that time by the military operations at City Point, sent the same to the State Department, where they were consigned to oblivion. On your memorialist's arrival home, he was further informed that Mr. Hale, encouraged by the impunity which his misdeeds had met in the hands of Mr. Seward, by another stretch of consular power and the usurpation of jurisdiction, attached and seized, and thereby prevented the sale of your memorialist's property, worth over $60,000, which he locked up so as to cause its destruction by dampness and rust, and prevented, also, the collection of over $40,000 duo him, and, in other words, totally ruined his business in Egypt. (See Appendix, p. 86, No. 69.) To give coloring to these high-handed acts, Mr. Hale alleged as excuse that he made that seizure with a view to protect a small claim of about £1,000, made up for the occasion by his New York friends, Messrs. R. H. Allen & Co., for whom he was acting as agent and attorney. Seize and put in jeopardy $100,000, without a shadow of authority, and without even taking security for damages in case of unlawful detention, on a mere excuse of protecting an alleged claim of £1,000, presented under the claimant's false oath, and *unsustained by proof ! ! !*

Allen & Co., the claimants, as well as your memorialist, were then and are now residents of and domiciled in the United States, and had the claim been just and genuine, as in fact it was unjust and spurious, its decision pertained to the regularly constituted courts of our common country, and not to the arbitrary, not to say interested, dictum of a consul in Egypt. His true object was to rob your memorialist, whom rumor in Egypt and here had reported dead or dying, and this charge is, moreover, sustained by the fact that his friends, the said Allens, about the same time sued for that same claim, upon a like false oath, before the Supreme Court of the District of Columbia, and levied attachment upon your memorialist's real estate in this city, but upon counsel's appearance and denial of the alleged debt, and demand for trial, Allen's attorney *dismissed the suit at their costs,* (see docket S. C. District Columbia, No. 1414,) thereby showing that they had no true claim!

Against Hale's usurpation of jurisdiction your memorialist complained to President Lincoln. The lamented President kindly promised to redress the wrong, but untimely death prevented his so doing.

Your memorialist next wrote and spoke to President Johnson, furnishing him a full report of the whole case. (See Appendix, pp. 81 & 83; Nos. 65 & 67.) But after renewed promises to look into it he has failed and neglected so to do. Your memorialist then, with a view to induce some action in his behalf, applied for an opinion, on Hale's assumption of jurisdiction, to the Justices of the Supreme Court of the District of Columbia, from before which the Allens had dismissed their suit to continue it before Hale in Egypt.

The Justices denied Hale's jurisdiction in the premises, styled his act "an usurpation," and declared him liable to damages. (See Appendix, page 86; No. 70.)

A certified copy of this opinion was handed to President Johnson by a distinguished member of the Cabinet, urging that, out of respect for that opinion, if for no other consideration, Hale be ordered to surrender the property so illegally seized by him; but the President answered that his own action in the premises may be distasteful to Mr. Seward, and he sent the opinion to the State Department, where, after various attempts to induce one of its signers to recon sider the same, it was disregarded by it and its protégé, Hale, to whom a copy was also sent, and who answered to those in Egypt remonstrating against his conduct, that nothing could hurt him or prevent his carrying out his schemes *while Mr.*

Seward lived, as he (Hale) was acting with his assent, and that no power could stand in his way.

With a view to sanction, (?) by an *ex post facto* law, Mr. Hale's usurpation of jurisdiction, and legalize his iniquity, the enactment by Congress of a law was pressed last July, the real object of which was studiously concealed. (*a*)

That law was approved July 28, 1866, and is appended as a section to the miscellaneous civil appropriation bill of first session Thirty-Ninth Congress, chap. 296, sec. 11; but it means nothing, because if in the European point of view Egypt is held as a part of the dominions of the Ottoman Porte, with which we have treaties, the acts of 11th August, 1848, and 22d June, 1860, *to carry into effect certain treaties*, and the 22d section of the former, and 21st section of the latter acts, extending in a limited degree the provisions of said acts to Turkey, give the United States consuls in Egypt all the powers necessary to carry out our treaties,

---

(*a*) The following appears in the Congressional Globe of July 25, 1866, viz:

Mr. SUMNER. I offer an amendment as an additional section, in which there is no appropriation:

And be it further enacted: That the provisions of the act to carry into effect the treaties between the United States and China, Japan, Siam, Persia, and other countries, giving certain judicial powers to ministers and consuls, or other functionaries of the United States in those countries, and for other purposes. approved June 22, 1860, shall extend to Egypt; and the consul general at Alexandria shall have the power provided by section twenty-two of such act for the consul general or the consul residing at the capital of a country where there is no minister.

I move this amendment under the direction of the Committee on Foreign Relations. I moved it last year, and the Senate adopted it on the appropriation bill, which, it will be remembered, failed. The object is simply to extend certain powers to our consul general at Alexandria which he has not now under the existing law.

Mr. SHERMAN. There are plenty of bills to which this would be more germane.

Mr. SUMNER. I beg the Senator's pardon. There is no other bill to come forward where it can be offered.

Mr. SHERMAN. Why has it not been presented before?

Mr. SUMNER. My attention was called to it only yesterday.

Mr. SHERMAN. When you kept quiet so long, there would seem to be no haste for putting it here. It is legislative in its character, purely.

Mr. SUMNER. What is the character of half of the propositions that have been voted on this bill?

Mr. SHERMAN. They were appropriations. This is the first one of this kind.

Mr. SUMNER. This was voted last year on the same appropriation bill. It is according to the usage of the Senate to make the appropriation bill the occasion for passing propositions like this which have been forgotten. My attention was called to this during this session for the first time yesterday.

The amendment was agreed to. (Congressional Globe, 1st session, 39th Congress, page 4,128.)

which, however, don't require them to assume jurisdiction upon matters between Americans resident in the United States, nor cover Hale's usurpation of such jurisdiction; and therefore the enactment aforestated was unnecessary. And on the other hand, if Mr. Seward's policy of 1861, alluded to in note (||) of p. 4 of this memorial be sustained by the United States Government, and Egypt is thereby to be considered *an independent power*, as we have no treaty with this *new power*, the enactment in question *extending to our consul there the benefit of acts passed to carry into effect existing treaties* becomes void and inoperative until a treaty with that *new power* be ratified.

Passing from the criminal to the ridiculous, Mr. Hale, through an adherent to his understanding of law, served upon your memorialist last August, at his residence in Washington city, two papers which he styled *summonses*, asking your memorialist to appear before him *in Egypt, to try the claims of the Allens, of New York!* And he appointed, also, one Mr. Choate, of New York, a commissioner to take testimony respecting that claim, with a *threat to your memorialist* that if he did not appear *his honor (?) would give judgment by default.* (See Appendix, pp. 87 and 88, Nos. 71 and 72.)

Whereupon, your memorialist, after making a last unsuccessful effort with President Johnson to check Mr. Hale's iniquities, applied to the Supreme Court of the State of New York, where said Choate and Allens reside, with prayer to enjoin and restrain him, his principal, and the latter's accomplices, from further prosecuting or proceeding before the self-constituted Judge Hale.

On the 31st of last August the Supreme Court granted your memoralist's prayer by a temporary injunction, and upon final hearing, ordered that *the said defendants Allen* "*be, and they are hereby, restrained and enjoined from further prosecuting or proceeding in any manner, either by themselves, their agents, servants, attorneys, or counsellors in the action or proceeding instituted by them before the defendant, Charles Hale, at Alexandria, in Egypt, against the plaintiff, or from authorizing, requesting, or directing said Hale to continue to keep possession, and from in any manner interfering with the property, credits, and effects of the said plaintiff at Alexandria aforesaid; and it is also ordered that the said defendant, Joseph H. Choate, be, and he is hereby, enjoined and restrained from summoning or examining any witnesses, or acting in any manner under the commission issued to him by said Charles Hale, to take testimony in the said proceedings instituted before him by said defendants Allen against said plaintiff.*" (See Appendix, page 89; Nos. 73—74.)

From this order the Allens appealed, and the court above confirmed, upon appeal, the decision of the court below, and by an opinion, in which the court was *unanimous*, denied Hale's jurisdiction. (See Appendix, page 90; No. 75.) But as Hale cannot be reached in Egypt by the process of the New York court, he continues to hold your memoralist's property, and to quietly enjoy the benefit of his plunder. And in this connection your memorialist shows, that although he has applied for the proper remedies of the law, and has through it established Hale's guilt and his liability to damages, still the law can afford him no full remedy from the fact: First, that Hale is without the jurisdiction of our courts; and, secondly, that the damages sustained by your memoralist exceed $100,000, whilst Mr. Hale's official bond secures him only in the sum of $10,000; and, therefore, that he has no other remedy for full relief but in the action of Congress.

Moreover, Mr. Seward directed the Fifth Auditor to decline refunding to your memorialist the amount which he has advanced for the support of the Consulate General in Alexandria, during the interim from Mr. Thayer's death to Charles Hale's arrival; and which is annually provided for by an express appropriation by Congress; nor to make for that interim the usual allowance established by precedents, alleging as reason *that no information had been given to the Department by Mr. Thayer on the subject, and that the assumption, by your memorialist, of the duties of the Consulate was not recognized by it.* This statement is refuted by the following facts:

First. That Mr. Thayer *did*, by his despatch, No. 38, dated September 5th, 1863, and forwarded through Mr. J. Miller, United States despatch agent, London, inform the Department of your memorialist's appointment as Acting Consul General until his return, (see Appendix, page 3; No. 4,) *and that he never* again resumed the duties of the office after that date.

Second. That Mr. Thayer *did*, by official circulars and commission, issued the same day, accredit and commission your memoralist to, and, that he was recognized by, the Egyptian Government and foreign representatives, and by our armed vessels, as the Acting United States Consul General, and that under these credentials these officials continued recognizing and transacting with him all their official business until the 19th of August, 1864, when he informed them of Charles Hale's appointment, and withdrew from the office, and these credentials and commission are on record among the archives of the Egyptian Government, the foreign representatives, the Consulate General, and your memorialist's papers, and are here reproduced in Appendix, pages 1–3; Nos. 1–5.

Third. That the State Department *did* receive Mr. Thayer's despatch, before alluded to, and twelve additional despatches from your memorialist, under his official signature as Acting Consul General, during the periods between September, 1863, and August, 1864, inclusive, all relating to the business of the consulate, among which that containing the valuable information of the proof obtained in the Birkenhead iron-clad case. That it never, during all that period, intimated to your memorialist its dissatisfaction of his acting as Consul General in Egypt; and that *its silence implied consent*, and *its use of his continued services established its recognition and sanction.*

Fourth. That Mr. Thayer's announcement to the State Department of his return to Egypt did not, in the least, change your memorialist's position in the face of the fact that, under the credentials before alluded to, which Mr. Thayer would not revoke until he could be able to resume the duties of the consulate, your memorialist uninterruptedly continued acting as Consul General, and was the only *de facto* representative of this Government in Egypt; and as Mr. Thayer died without resuming the duties of that office, and without revoking these credentials, no further or other information from him could have become necessary, unless, indeed, Mr. Seward expected him to inform the Department of his own death and of your memorialist's continuation in the consulate.

If Mr. S. had not meant to recognize your memorialist as the Acting Consul General, he ought, upon the receipt of the information thereof, to have notified him that his services were dispensed with. He could not use those services during twelve months, and after reaping their benefit, come out with the language before quoted, or try to ignore your memorialist. Indeed this latter scheme was adopted only at a subsequent period, when Mr. Seward, in consequence of your memorialist's firm attitude in the cases before referred to, was placed in a position to accept the alternative of sustaining national rights, or his favorite, Mr. Hale. He chose the latter.

To carry out like policy, it was settled that the Egyptian government was in no event to be displeased by the pursual of a too resolute defence of American rights, while at the same time it became necessary to disavow your memorialist and his acts, and to sustain Hale's course in rehoisting our flag without redress, in declining its protection to those entitled to it against the most urgent appeals for justice, and in suffocating with inflexible hand every claim arising from the arbitrary acts of the Egyptian government. It would also be necessary to nullify the decided steps which your memorialist had alraady taken in behalf of American interests, and bury all attending circumstances in diplomatic oblivion ; to treat that class of rights as non-existent, and to declare that your memorialist had no authority to move in their defense or in behalf of any American cause whatever, and in that way completely dispose of all existing complications and close the door to future discussion or reclamation.

But Mr. Seward forgot that the success of such policy required two things, which cannot well be accomplished—the first, to obliterate your memorialist's credentials, which *prove that he had that authority ;* and the second, which is most important and conclusive, to strike out of existence *Mr. Thayer's instructions urging your memorialist in the course which he pursued.*

Whereupon, respectfully submitting for the consideration of Congress the many unlawful acts here stated, committed by Mr. Hale with Mr. Seward's connivance, your memorialist prays for such legislation in the premises as will vindicate the honor of our flag, and give security to the rights of American citizens residing in Egypt. And your memorialist further prays for the restoration of his property, unlawfully seized by Mr. Hale and still unlawfully detained by him, in violation of the order of injunction made by the Supreme Court of the State of New York, and for the damages resulting from such unlawful seizure and detention; together with such other and further relief as justice and equity may require.

F. DAINESE.

WASHINGTON, D. C., 26*th December*, 1866.

ERRATA.

Page 15, No. 16.—For Despatch No. 140, read No. 40.
26, No. 27.—For Teki Bey, read Zeki Bey.
36, No. 37.—For Mondios, read Modinos.
43.—For Tastio, read Tastu.

APPENDIX.

CREDENTIALS.

No. 1.

Mr. Thayer to the Egyptian Government.

(Translated copy.)

AGENCY AND CONSULATE GENERAL OF THE
UNITED STATES OF AMERICA IN EGYPT,
ALEXANDRIA, *5th Sept.*, 1863.

EXCELLENCY:

I have the honor to bring to your knowledge that my Government having granted me a leave, Mr. Francis Dainese remains, during my absence, chargé to conduct all the business of this office.

I have the honor to renew to your Excellency the assurance of my high consideration.

(Signed) W. S. THAYER,
Consul General.

To His Excellency CHERIF PACHA,
Minister for Foreign Affairs of his Highness the Viceroy of Egypt.

As Mr. Thayer died without ever making his return officially known, the Egyptian government, and all others in Egypt, recognized Mr. Dainese as Acting Consul General from the date of this credential until his notice of withdrawal on the 19th August, 1864.

No. 2.

Mr. Thayer to Mr. Tastu.

(Circular—Translated Copy.)

AGENCY AND CONSULATE GENERAL OF THE
UNITED STATES OF AMERICA IN EGYPT,
ALEXANDRIA, *5th September*, 1863.

SIR:

I have the honor to bring to your knowledge that having received a leave from my Government, Mr. Francis Dainese remains, during my absence, chargê to conduct all the business of this office.

I have the honor to renew to you the assurance of my high consideration.

(Signed) W. S. THAYER,
Consul General.

To Mr. TASTU,
Agent and Consul General of France in Egypt.

A similar Circular was sent to all the diplomatic and consular bodies in Egypt, and other authorities.

No. 3.

Mr. Thayer to Captains of armed vessels and others.

AGENCY AND CONSULATE GENERAL OF THE
UNITED STATES OF AMERICA IN EGYPT,
ALEXANDRIA, *Sept.* 5, 1863.

I hereby authorize and appoint Francis Dainese, esq., during my absence, to conduct in my place the affairs of this office, and hereby request all commanders and captains of vessels, armed or unarmed, as well as all other persons, to recognize and consider the said Francis Dainese accordingly.

[L. S.] In witness whereof I have hereunto set my hand and affixed my seal of office on the day and year above written.

(Signed) W. S. THAYER,
Consul General.

No. 4.

Mr. Thayer to Mr. Seward.

[No. 38.] U. S. CONSULATE GENERAL,
ALEXANDRIA, *Sept.* 5, 1863.

SIR:

I gratefully accept the month's respite granted to me by you, and during my absence I authorize Mr. Francis Dainese of Washington City, to assume charge of the Consulate General and to act as my exclusive representative in office.

I have the honor to be very respectfully, sir,

Your obedient servant,
(Signed) W. S. THAYER.
Consul General.

Hon. W. H. SEWARD,
Secretary of State, Washington, D. C.

No. 5.

Mr. Thayer to Cherif Pasha.

(Translated Copy.)

ALEXANDRIA, *Sept.* 5, 1863.

EXCELLENCY:

A severe illness which obliges me to leave immediately, deprives me of the pleasure of shaking hands with you previous to my departure.

I must then content myself with sending you my cordial farewell by my friend, Mr. Dainese, whom I leave in my place, and whom I recommend most especially to you.

Mr. Dainese is a friend of many years' standing, and respected everywhere in my country as a man who is as honorable and just as he is capable and skillful.

Permit me to beg your Excellency that none other but him be allowed to approach His Highness, or your Ministry, as my representative.

Your devoted,
(Signed) WM. S. THAYER.

His Excellency CHERIF PASHA,
Minister for Foreign Affairs,

No. 6.

Mr. Thayer to Mr. Dainese.

ALEXANDRIA, *Sept.* 4, 1863

MY DEAR DAINESE:

I wish you, during my absence, to exercise the fullest authority, according to your judgment, in which I have the greatest confidence.

Among other things, I desire that during my absence you restore the former state of things, and make the Cairo "proteges" entirely dependent on the Consulate General at Alexandria. Let them receive their permits of residence here, have all their Consular or legal business transacted here, and all their petitions and acts transmitted through the medium of this Consulate General.

Excuse my rheumatic writing, if the sense is clear—what I mean is to confide all to your discretion.

Your friend,
(Signed) W. S. THAYER.

FRANCIS DAINESE, Esq.

IRON-CLAD RAMS.

No. 7.

Mr. Dainese to Mr. Seward.

[No. 39.] U. S. CONSULATE GENERAL,
ALEXANDRIA, *Sept.* 11, 1863.

SIR:

I have the honor to inform the Department, that in consequence of telegrams and letters received at this office from our Minister at London, and our Consul at Liverpool, respecting the building at Birkenhead of two iron-clads, supposed to be for the Confederates, the ownership whereof is attributed to the Egyptian government, I applied to, and obtained from that government an official denial of its having anything to do, or being in any way concerned with the same, and have instantly conveyed by telegraph this invaluable information to Mr. Adams, to whom I now send by mail a copy of the despatch. In granting my request H. H. reiterated his expressions of friendship for our Government, adding that he was happy to have it in his power to place in its hands a proof whereby to baffle the efforts of its enemies.

I am, sir, very respectfully,
Your obedient servant,
(Signed) F. DAINESE,
Acting Consul General.

Hon. W. H. SEWARD,
Secretary of State.

The Viceroy denied the ownership of these rams in an official letter of the following purport, written in French, through his Minister, dated the 8th, but received by the Consulate the 11th September, 1863, viz:

No. 8.

Cherif Pasha to Mr. Dainese.

(Translated Copy.)

[No. 722.] DEPARTMENT OF FOREIGN AFFAIRS,
Alexandria, 8th Sept., 1863.

SIR:

I have received the despatch which you did me the honor to address to me, informing me that the Messrs. Laird were engaged in building two iron-clad frigates which they pretend to be destined to the government of H. H. the Viceroy, and asking whether this government had really ordered the same.

In reply I hereby inform you that this government is *entirely* stranger to the building you mention, and moreover that it does not recognize any order whatexer of that nature.

Accept, sir, the assurance of my high consideration.

(Signed) CHERIF PASHA,
Minister for Foreign Affairs.

F. DAINESE, Esq.,
U. S. Acting Consul General.

The telegram sent by Mr. Dainese to Mr. Adams, upon receipt of the above, is substantially as follows:

No. 9.

Mr. Dainese to Mr. Adams.

U. S. Consulate General,
Alexandria, 11th Sept., 1863.

Hon Francis Adams,
U. S. Minister Plenipotentiary, &c., &c., London.

The Egyptian government officially denied the ownership of, and all concern with, the Birkenhead iron-clads. Despatch per mail. F. DAINESE.

By the following mail Mr. Dainese forwarded to Mr. Adams the paper in due form, at the same time informing Mr. Thayer and Mr. Bigelow, at Paris, of the occurrence.

Subsequently Mr. Dainese received the following, viz:

No. 10.

Mr. Thayer to Mr. Dainese.

Paris, 22d Sept., 1863.

Your letter, with Cherif Pasha's note, was invaluable, and has given us great satisfaction. Could you add to our pleasure and climax the matter by getting an official refutation of the report here circulated that the Viceroy has promised to look at the two iron-clads ordered by Bravet if they come to Alexandria, with a view of purchasing them, and in case of not purchasing them, to assist Bravet in selling them to the Sultan. You know Bravet claims the two frigates as his own and demands, as a French subject, that his government shall release them; but his government refuses, saying there is no evidence that he owns them. My opinion, therefore, is that this report is designed by Bravet to induce England to let the frigates go, as if to the Mediterranean, so that he can easily deliver them to the Confederates. * * * * *

(Signed) W. S. THAYER.

Francis Dainese, Esq.,
Acting Consul General of the U. S. of America,
Alexandria, Egypt.

Upon receipt of the above message, and another on the following October from Mr. Bigelow, then our Consul at Paris, Mr. Dainese got from the Egyptian government the desired refutation; transmitted it in official form for the use of our Legations in Paris and London, and brought the fact to the knowledge of the State Department in his despatch, as follows, viz:

No. 11.

Mr. Dainese to Mr. Seward.

[No. 41] U. S. CONSULATE GENERAL,
ALEXANDRIA, *Oct.* 27, 1863.

SIR: Since this government's official denial, telegraphed by me to Mr. Adams the 11th of last Sept., of its ownership of the iron-clads at Birkenhead, and the seizure of these vessels, it has been asserted, evidently with a view to procure their release, that they were the property of Mr. Bravet, a French merchant, who was invited by H. Highness, the Viceroy, to bring them here, and was promised their purchase, or a recommendation to His Imperial Majesty, the Sultan, to take them.

I lost no time in bringing this new plea to the knowledge of His Highness, and asking an official contradiction of this assertion, which I have obtained and forwarded to our Ministers at Paris and London, and I submit the fact to the Department for its information.

I have the honor to be, &c., &c.,

F. DAINESE,
Acting Consul General.

Hon. W. H. SEWARD,
Secretary of State.

On the 26th December, 1863, Mr. Dainese wrote to Mr. Dudley, in reply to new inquiries on the subject of these rams, the memorandum which follows, viz:

The British government has been fully informed by its Agent and Consul General here of all the dates and details of the Viceroy's and Bravet's connection with the iron-clads. The Viceroy refused, from the beginning, to accept the rams, and in August last, Bravet signed a paper releasing His Highness from all obligation to take them. If the Sultan wishes to take them the British government has authorized an agent of its own to do so for him. It will hardly be necessary to send confirmation of these facts which are well established already to the British authorities.

ADAMI CASE.

No. 12.

Mr. Dainese to Mr. Seward.

[No. 40.] U. S. CONSULATE GENERAL,
ALEXANDRIA, *6th October*, 1863.

SIR: Herewith I have the honor to transmit copies of correspondence between this office and the British authorities at this place, relative to a case which has attracted considerable attention. * * * * * *

Hoping the United States Government will approve of my course, I have the honor to be, sir, very respectfully, your obedient servant,

(Signed,) F. DAINESE,
Acting Consul General.

Hon. W. H. SEWARD,
Secretary of State.

No. 13.

Mr. Dainese to Mr. Colquhoun.

ALEXANDRIA, *18th September*, 1863.

SIR: The person named Paraschiva Adami, an American protégé, under trial before the American consular court for offences of a serious nature, has just handed me the inclosed paper, which purports to be a protection from the British court, by virtue whereof he claims to have, since yesterday, obtained British protection.

From an examination of the records, I find that from 1857 to this date P. Adami has been under, and has enjoyed, American protection, always acknowledging himself an American protégé; that he committed, while under that protection the offences for which he has been tried; that he was arrested as an American protégé, signed his bail, and attended his trial at the American consular court *as such;* and, as is natural and in harmony with existing laws and practices, he must abide, *as such*, by the decision of said court.

It being evident that he begged for British protection in the hope to screen himself from justice, and that the ignorance of his purpose has alone induced the granting of such protection, I deem it proper to return to you the paper in question, and to request that you be so kind as to inform of the facts here stated the officers of the British court, and other officers connected with your agency and consulate general, that they may not, through mistake, give further assistance to P. Adami.

I have the honor to be, sir, very respectfully, your obedient servant,

(Signed,) F. DAINESE,
Acting Consul General.

Hon. Mr. COLQUHOUN,
H. B. M. Agent and Consul General for Egypt.

No. 14.

Mr. Fonblanque to Mr. Dainese.

BRITISH CONSULAR COURT FOR EGYPT,
ALEXANDRIA, 21*st September*, 1863.

SIR: I had hoped that the result of our conversation on Friday last would have been the release from custody of Paraschiva Adami, an Ionian citizen, the bearer of a British certificate of registration, granted by this court. I have yet to learn in what capacity and under what circumstances Adami became entitled to American protection.

This person, as I had the honor to inform you, applied to me for his certificate in March last, when Her Majesty's order in council, rendering registration imperative upon her subjects, came into operation; but not being provided with all the necessary papers his registration was postponed till he could produce them.

It must, therefore, be considered that any temporary protection which, rightly or wrongly, he might have previously enjoyed, was, *de facto*, renounced when he applied to this court to be recognized in his proper character as an Ionian.

His papers, as such, were presented on the 17th September, when he was placed upon our register and granted his certificate.

It is deeply to be regretted that a person in possession of so conclusive and regular a document should have been arrested by a foreign authority—the more so as there appears not to be the slightest ground to believe he intended to quit this city.

As Paraschiva Adami applied in March to be officially recognized as a British subject, the contention that he merely sought our protection to evade the effect of proceedings which commenced in the following August, falls to the ground.

The fact remains that this man is imprisoned in the loathsome jail of the Zaptieh by your orders, after having shown to you and to the local authorities his certificate of registration as a British subject; and you must pardon my observing that every hour his incarceration continues gives weight to the reparation which will certainly be demanded of every person concerned in his arrest.

I trust you will see the propriety of ordering his immediate release; and when this is effected I shall be happy to confer with you as to what means should be taken for securing justice to any one whom he may have wronged.

I have the honor to be, your obedient, humble servant,

(Signed,) ALBANY FONBLANQUE,
Her Britannic Majesty's Legal Vice-Consul.

To Francis Dainese, Esq.,
Act'g Ag't and Con. Gen. of the U. S. A. in Egypt.

No. 15.

Dainese to Mr. Fonblanque.

U. S. Consulate General,
Alexandria, *September* 28, 1863.

Sir: I had hoped that the facts stated in my despatch of 18th instant, would have suggested to you the propriety of not interfering in favor of Pavaschiva Adami, an American protégé, tried and sentenced by the American consular court.

However, in your communication of 21st inst., received the 23d, and that of 23d received on the 24th, you claim this person, first, as an "Ionian," then, as a "British subject," and request to be informed "in what capacity and under what circumstances Adami became entitled to American protection;" also of "the date of his last registration."

In reply, I will briefly state, that on April 3, 1857, P. Adami acknowledged, under his signature to be a native-born Smirniote, therefore a Turkish Greek. That, being then 27 years old—under public law giving all men of age the right of changing nationality, (Fœlix Droit, Interna'l Privé, book 1, title 1, page 55)—he begged for, and, by a certificate of that date, was received under American protection; his last certificate as permit of residence is for the year 1863.

It is well known that, by the laws of Turkey, Foreign Consuls have a right to extend protection; and it is equally known by public law, that an alien or a stranger born, for so long a time as he continues under the protection of a Foreign Government, owes obedience to the laws of that Government, and may be punished for crimes *as a native-born* subject might be. This principle is sanctioned by all modern legislators and publicists, and is faithfully observed by the Government I have the honor to represent. If quotations be necessary, I refer among others, to Fœlix's Droit International Privé, book 2, title 9, chap. 4, § 599; also to extracts from opinions of eminent jurists, reported in Wheaton's Elements of International Law, 6th edition, page 122 and sequel. In page 135 of the latter work, the principle is thus stated:

"By the laws of Turkey and other Eastern nations, the consulates therein may receive under their protection strangers and sojourners whose religion and social manners do not assimilate with the religion and manners of those countries. The persons thus received become thereby invested with the nationality of the protecting consulate. International law recognizes and sanctions the rights acquired by this connection." The same principle was adhered to by the Lords of Appeals in the High Court of Admiralty in England *in their* decision "that a merchant carrying on trade at Smyrna, under the protection of a Dutch consul, was to be considered a Dutchman as to his national character." (Wheaton's International Law, 3d edition, page 384).

Under this principle, Adami having voluntarily adopted American nationality, having continued under it and enjoyed its benefits, and having, while in the enjoyment of these benefits, offended American law, been tried, and sentenced therefor, he must continue under that nationality until he has fulfilled the decrees of its court; and he cannot be permitted to throw up his temporary allegiance to the United States and adopt British nationality before such fulfilment has been accomplished.

You will thus perceive, sir, that P. Adami is not—as you say —a British subject; that you can have no founded right to claim him as such; that the *plea* in your communication of 21st inst., to the effect *that his application to your court to be recognized as an "Ionian" is a* DE FACTO *renunciation of the temporary protection which "rightly or wrongly" he might have previously enjoyed*—is untenable, such renunciation not being receivable until after the fulfilment of his obligations towards the protecting power; and that your conclusions and demands resting on that plea "fall to the ground;" and, in this connection, I may be permitted to observe that, even admitting the material fact set forth by you, of Adami's application last March to be recognized as an Ionian, judicially speaking, such application ought on the same day to have been communicated to the American authority by both your court and Adami; inasmuch as to that authority the application counts only from the 18th of September, the day on which he exhibited the certificate you gave him on the day before; and on that day it was too late, the American court having already proceeded against him.

But aside of international right, which fully disposes of this question, and upon which I plant myself, let it be remembered that both public report and the Ionian laws render doubtful at this time Adami's claim to British protection: First, because it is asserted that the papers by virtue whereof he claims it *are not* those of his ancestors; and this assertion acquired credibility from Adami's written acknowledgment of being a native-born Smirniote; from his living as a Turkish Greek until he became clothed with American nationality; and from the fact, most remarkable, that when he could live no longer here without protection, instead of resorting to his *now alleged right* to British, he begged for and was granted American protection—all which goes to show that the claim is made up by him to serve his unsuccessful attempt of flying from justice. Secondly, because, even if those papers were rightly his, their filing, *only since last March at a British court at Alexandria*, is not in accordance with the requirements of articles 21 to 23 of the "Civil Code of Ionian Islands," (Book 1, title 1, chapter 1, page 4,) which demand a year's previous application *at a court of the Regency*, before the claim can be admitted; and further, that even if Adami were rightly admitted as an Ionian, the Ionian laws adhere to the right of expatriation, (same code, chapter 2, section 30, page 5,) and, as a consequence, to the principle of the expatriated party's duty *to fulfil its obligations towards its formerly* adopted nationality.

Taking your remark respecting imprisonment in a "loathsome jail," as the dictates of a good heart's sympathies, and not as argument against said imprisonment, I will observe that it became imperative under the statute, upon the evidence of his intention to evade, exhibited in his disobedience to the American court, on the plea that he was no longer an American but a British subject. But a glance at his offence of intentionally deceiving, and, under most aggravating circumstances, seducing and ruining the future of an honest, innocent young woman, almost a child, and an orphan, will make him unworthy of sympathy. He can come out of that jail by complying with his sentence, and I am credibly informed that he would have willingly complied with it but for the lures of British protection.

As I had the honor already of observing to you, our respective positions impose upon us the duty to repress wrongs. If criminals under your jurisdiction should seek under the "stars and stripes" a shelter against punishment, I should deny it; I am entitled to, and I trust in, full reciprocity on your part.

Under all these circumstances, and after due consideration of the subject, I feel satisfied that I would be unjustifiable and be acting inconsistently with my duty to my Government and country were I to comply with your request of *releasing* P. Adami, before full compliance with the sentence passed upon him by the U. S. consular court, or of *recognizing* his alleged change of nationality before his allegiance to the United States has ceased to exist; and this allegiance cannot cease without his proper discharge, which he cannot obtain without compliance with said sentence.

With regard to your quotation of Mr. Saunder's circular, not on file at this office, that "the chiefs of foreign consulates are requested to communicate directly with me (you) in all matters relating to the administration of justice," permit me to observe that the subject of this correspondence, being one of international right, does not seem to come within the sense of that circular.

Nevertheless, since both yourself and Mr. Colquhoun wish that the same be treated directly with you, I cheerfully comply with your request to address this directly to you, and will thank you to convey its contents to Mr. Colquhoun.

As to sending you a copy of the original complaint, I can see no good reason for it—that paper, with all the others, having already in open trial been considered before the United States court, which alone was competent to take cognizance thereof, and whose judgments are not subject to the revisions of any foreign court.

I have the honor to be, sir, your obedient and humble servant,

(Signed) F. DANIESE,
Acting Consul General.

ALBANY FONBLANQUE, Esq.,
Her Britannic Majesty's Legal Vice-Consul for Egypt.

No. 16.

Mr. Dainese to Mr. Seward.

[No. 42.] U. S. CONSULATE GENERAL,
ALEXANDRIA, *November* 12, 1863.

SIR: I have the honor to inform the Department that P. Adami, the correspondence in whose case was transmitted to you in my dispatch No. 140, has this day complied with the sentence passed upon him by the American consular court, and been released by order of said court.

In a respectful petition addressed to this office, he acknowledges his wrong in trying to fly American justice under British colors, confessing that he was induced to it by bad advice, and the facilities shown him by the British authorities; and he now tells publicly that American laws made him a better man, and that he will stand by them forever. Thus has terminated the affair.

In am, very respectfully, sir, your obedient servant,

F. DAINESE,
Actirg Consul General.

HON. W. H. SEWARD,
Secretary of State.

No. 17.

Mr. Thayer to Mr. Dainese.

PARIS, *October* 20, 1863.

I have read your budget of despatches (on the Adami

case) *with entire approval, and have written so to Mr. Seward.* They have been all forwarded. I am very happy that you have so distinguished yourself. Mr. Bigelow thinks your argument conclusive.

I congratulate you on the ability with which you have conducted the affair. I am sure the reputation of the consulate will be greatly raised by it.

(Signed) W. S. THAYER.

FRANCIS DAINESE, Esq.,
Act'g Consul Gen'l of the U. S. A., Alexandria, Egypt.

AMERICAN CLAIMS.

No. 18.

Mr. Thayer to Mr. Dainese.

PARIS, *September* 29, 1863.

* * * * Make all the appointments to consular agencies before my return. * * * * *

(Signed) W. S. THAYER.

FRANCIS DAINESE, Esq.,
Act'g Consul Gen'l of the U. S. A., Alexandria, Egypt.

No. 19.

Mr. Thayer to Mr. Dainese.

PARIS, *October* 12, 1863.

* * * Please talk fully to the Viceroy on our protégé's affairs, and persecute him until he fixes some arrangement. Nothing but solicitation will do it. * * *

I hope you will not hesitate to use all the powers you possess to punish any refractory agent. Do everything that is just and expedient, nothing more, nothing less. What that is you can judge on the ground better than I here. But when you have calmly made up your mind don't hesitate to enforce your opinion, and I will sustain it.

(Signed) W. S. THAYER.

FRANCIS DAINESE, Esq.,

Act'g Consul Gen'l of the U. S. A., Alexandria, Egypt.

Agreeable to the above instructions of Mr. Thayer, Mr. Dainese made the necessary appointments to consular agencies, and pressed the American claims, which necessitated, besides numerous verbal applications, also his writing to the Egyptian Government a great number of despatches, among which are the following:

No. 20.

Mr. Dainese to Cherif Pacha.

[Translated Copy.]

U. S. CONSULATE GENERAL IN EGYPT,
ALEXANDRIA, *October* 26, 1863.

EXCELLENCY: I have the honor to transmit to you herewith a request of Mr. G. Anhuri, bearing date the 19th inst.; a second from Mr. Saba Ascaros Cassis, of the 22d ditto; a third from Mr. Wassif el Hayat, our agent at Siout, dated the 23d, and a fourth from Messrs. G. and T. Kindineco, of the 24th of the same month; to the contents of which I invite your attention.

Hoping that justice will be done to the petitioners, I have the honor to renew to your Excellency the assurance of my high consideration.

(Signed) F. DAINESE.
Acting Consular General.

To His Excellency CHERIF PACHA,
Minister for Foreign Affairs.

No. 21.

Mr. Dainese to Cherif Pacha.

[Translated Copy.]

U. S. CONSULATE GENERAL IN EGYPT,
ALEXANDRIA, *November* 2, 1863.

EXCELLENCY: I have the honor to transmit herewith a request addressed to me by Mr. Abellana, an American citizen but recently arrived in Egypt, from whom the railway officials have unjustly taken piastres 510, and to whom his excellency the Governor of Alexandria refuses to do justice, on the pretence that the seizure was authorized by the regulations of the railway, which forbids the carrying of money by passengers.

Apart from the injustice of pretending that a traveler is not allowed to carry in his purse the small sum of 100 napoleons, you will admit, Mr. le Minister, that a stranger newly arrived in Egypt cannot be expected to know all the regulations which it may please each company to make, and which, in any case, would, as far as they disagreed with common law, only be applicable to residents.

Our American companies have likewise their special regulations, but there is no example extant of a stranger injured by their rules not having obtained justice before the courts of law. It is this justice which His Excellency the Governor of Alexandria has denied to the above mentioned American citizen: and I am compelled to state with regret that I am unacquainted with a single case in which he has granted to our fellow-citizens the attention which I have the right to expect from the functionaries of the enlightened government of His Highness the Viceroy.

Hoping that you will issue the necessary orders, to the effect that justice be done to Mr. Abellana, and that due attention be paid in future by the Governor of Alexandria to applications from this office, I have the honor to renew to your Excellency assurance of my high consideration.

(Signed) F. DAINESE,
Acting Consul General.

To His Excellency CHERIF PACHA,
Minister for Foreign Affairs.

No. 22.

Mr. Dainese to Cherif Pacha.

[Translated Cop .]

CONSULATE GENERAL OF THE U. S. IN EGYPT,
ALEXANDRIA, *November* 4, 1863.

EXCELLENCY: I received this morning the despatch No. 825, which you did me the honor to address me under date of 31st of October last, and which inaugurates a new principle, at the same time that it affects both the rights and the privileges of this agency, and seems to ignore even its character towards the Egyptian Government. If this despatch be construed upon its letter, my only alternative would be to refer the matter to His Highness the Viceroy, and await his action. As, however, the friendly relations, both public and private, which exist between us, do not allow me to believe that it expresses your real intentions, and as the sentiments contained in your note of the 2d instant,* persuade me still more that the true bearing of the said despatch has escaped your attention, I have deemed it my duty, before taking any other step, to make the following observations to you, and to await your explanations.

I must first remind your Excellency that the Government of the United States of America looks upon Egypt, so far as its administration is concerned, as a separate State, governed by itself; and that it has, in consequence, accredited to it an agent direcly, not through an intermediary. Therefore, your suggestion in said despatch, that I ask through the channel of the embassy at Constantinople, that which I have a right to call for directly from the Egyptian Government, can only be construed into an abandonment by the latter of its rights, or to a want of courtesy to the agent accredited to it.

The simple fact of the existence of your department, and of the transaction of Egyptian affairs directly between that department and the foreign representatives residing here,

*Cherif Pacha's note of 2d November, 1853, above referred, is here produced, to fortify Mr. Dainese's position, in supposing that the bearing of the despatch of 31st October must have escaped the Minister's attention.

disposes negatively of the former; and this is still better illustrated by your recent action in the matter of the measures of police, for the adoption of which you deemed it necessary to ask our concurrence, and not that of the Sublime Porte, or of the embassadors at Constantinople.

Viewing the question on the second point, it would appear to assume a character which would call for the action of the Government of Washington. Without wishing to discuss here the question of Mr. Rahmi's nomination, who, by the bye, is not a native of Egypt, but a Russo-Circassian, and long since an American protégé, permit me to observe that this agency possesses the right, undisputed until now, to select its "employés," even amongst the natives, and that it is only aware of the rule you mention, as forming part of the news in a newspaper. I can only, then, take cognizance of that rule after your department shall have made it the subject of an official communication, and can only adopt it when the American Government shall have approved of it.

If, as you say, this regulation has been adopted in Turkey, the article 3 thereof, invoked by you would, in this case, be applicable to the consulates and vice-consulates established in the portion of the Ottoman territory administered by the "employés" of the Sublime Porte, and which offices are dependent on the embassy at Constantinople, and are recognized by means of a "Berat" (exequatur) obtained through that embassy.

As Egypt has a separate administration, its prince and the foreign representatives at his court stand in their respective positions on the footing of the Porte with reference to the ministers accredited to it. Therefore, whenever the Egyptian Government shall have caused within its territory the adoption of the regulation in question, the article 3, of which you speak of, will then become applicable to the vice-consulates and consular agents in Egypt, named by this agency, recognized upon its direct application to your ministry, and which, being dependant on the said agency, must, of necessity, apply to it, in order to obtain from your ministry the authorization which like officers established in Turkey obtain through the channel of the embassy at the Sublime Porte. But for what concerns this agency, itself the highest authority accredited to the Egyptian Government, it ought not to address itself to any other but the latter, for the grant of the privileges and immunities guaranteed to it by treaties, international right, and custom, and I will consider all refusals on the part of the said government to grant them as a violation of its rights.

Inviting your most particular attention to these observations, I have the honor to renew to your excellency the assurance of my high consideration.

(Signed) F. DAINESE,
Acting Consul General.

To his Excellency CHERIF PACHA,
Minister for Foreign Affairs.

No. 23.

Cherif Pacha to Mr. Dainese.

[Translated Copy.]

CAIRO, *November* 2, 1863.

MR. ACTING CONSUL GENERAL:

I have received the note which you addressed me on the 30th ult., to inform me of the means you had adopted for the enforcement of the police measures stated in my circular of the 22d of same month.

I fully appreciate, Mr. Acting Consul General, the opportuneness and wisdom of the adoption of those means, and am very thankful to you for your ready support to the local authority on this occasion.

It is by thus uniting our efforts that we will succeed to attain the end, and to stop a state of things, the continuation of which would be very dangerous to public security.

Pray accept, Mr. Acting Consul General, the assurance of my high consideration.

(Signed) CHERIF PACHA,
Minister for Foreign Affairs.

F. DAINESE, Esq.,
Acting Consul General of the United States of America.

No. 24.

Mr. Dainese to Cherif Pacha.

[Translated Copy.]

U. S. Consulate General,
Alexandria, *November* 14, 1863.

Excellency: I have received the despatch which you have done me the honor of addressing me under date the 9th inst., in answer to mine of the 4th, from which I perceive that there has been a misconstruction on your part of the observations contained in the latter as relating to my Dragoman, Mr. Rahmi.

The employment and protection of this latter are foreign to the principle under discussion, and what I have said bears only on the respective positions of the Government of His Highness the Viceroy, towards the representatives accredited to him, and the privileges and immunities of this agency, amongst which is the right of employing natives, which right is ignored in your despatch of the 31st of last October.

In your despatch of 9th November, you admit the power of His Highness' Government to agree directly with foreign representatives for the adoption of police measures applicable in Egypt, and your ministry's previous despatches show that it has in fact exercised this power very rightfully, for everything regarding the Egyptian administration.

In view of this fact, I cannot explain how you can deny its power, I may even say its obligation, to make direct arrangements with the said representatives for the appointment of consular agents, required to enforce the observance of said measures by foreigners established or travelling in Egypt.

You ground your objection on the theory that the consular employment of a native produces an absolute change in his nationality, for which, say you, the sanction of the sovereign himself would be necessary; but this theory is upset by the fact that it only affords to the individual employed temporary privileges, which cease with the employment.

Even if that theory were correct, is not the sovereign's sanction to the Viceroy to dispose of his Egyptian subjects an acquired fact? and has he not already proved it to be so by making over six hundred armed Arabs to the Emperor of the French?

But, as you have raised all these objections on the strength of the alleged existence of a new regulation which I ignore, I shall refrain discussing its bearing until it is adopted and until it is officially communicated to me.

Permit me also to observe that, even if, as you say, a convention to that effect had been concluded between the Porte and the foreign legations at Constantinople, as an agreement with a minister is not binding upon his sovereign until he has ratified it, (Vatel, book 4, chap. 6, sec. 67,) such a convention cannot possibly, before its ratification, affect our relations, which must continue on the old footing, according to which I must insist on the right of employing natives when they have no suit or claim against the Egyptian Government.

Moreover, this privilege of employing natives is so well established and so constantly practised by every foreign representative in Egypt, that to deny it to the agent of the United States would be to manifest towards him dispositions not harmonizing with those which His Highness entertains for my Government.

As your declaration in the said despatch to the effect that His Highness the Viceroy is merely "a simple administrator," and not "the depositary of a part of the prerogatives of the Ottoman Empire," is susceptible of misconstruction and misinterpretation respecting the rights guaranteed to him by the European Powers, I beg you will explain the same, that I may, if necessary, make the fact known to my Government.

Your high intelligence and strict adherence to international law, assure me in advance that you will maintain the good understanding which should guide our relations, and conform to the suggestions in my despatch of the 4th inst.

I have the honor to renew to your excellency the assurance of my high consideration.

(Signed) F. DAINESE,
Acting Consul General.

To His Excellency CHERIF PACHA,
Minister of Foreign Affairs.

No. 25.

Mr. Dainese to Cherif Pacha.

[Translated Copy.]

U. S. CONSULATE GENERAL IN EGYPT,
ALEXANDRIA, *December* 12, 1863.

EXCELLENCY: I received, on my return here, the despatch No. 878, dated November 29, which you did me the honor of addressing me, from which I understand that, while you admit my theory of the powers attributed to His Highness the Viceroy, which the language of your letter No. 844, quoted in my note of November 14, had the appearance of limiting, you maintain that these powers do not reach so far as to enable His Highness to dispense with the application in Egypt of regulations of the existence of which I have been until now unaware, and which you state to have emanated from the Sublime Porte with reference to consular employments; whereupon I take the liberty of observing that, by the treaty of 1840, the laws of the Ottoman Empire are to be applied to Egypt, with such modifications as the difference of localities renders expedient; and that the expediency of these modifications is left to the judgment of His Highness the Viceroy, who has, moreover, the right of applying these laws in such manner as he may think fit.

If the convention on which the regulations seem to be based were ratified, their application to Egypt would, at all events, be subject to the modifications before stated; but, in any case, they cannot be applied in advance of its adoption, as the theory you put forth upon the supposed employment of a native asserts.

For these reasons I consider myself bound to continue to adhere to the principles laid down in my preceding letters of the 4th and 14th November.

As concerns Mr. Rahmi, I consider him foreign to the subject in discussion, because it only relates to principle, and not to the individual; moreover, after our conversation held at Cairo, subsequent to the above-mentioned despatch, I have reason to believe in your full acquiescence to that principle.

Accept, Excellency, the assurance of my high consideration.

(Signed) F. DAINESE,
Acting Consul General.

To His Excellency CHERIF PACHA,
Minister for Foreign Affairs.

No. 26.

Mr. Dainese to Cherif Pacha.

[Translated Copy.]

U. S. CONSULATE GENERAL IN EGYPT,
ALEXANDRIA, *January* 20, 1864.

EXCELLENCY: In my despatch of the 26th of October last, I had the honor to transmit a request from Messrs. George and Thomas Kindineco. Your ministry has not answered the said despatch.

I have the honor herewith to transmit the enclosed additional request from these gentlemen, who complain, and, I must say, with reason, of your silence.

Inviting the attention of the Egyptian Government to the complaints of those whose interests I am bound to press, I renew to your Excellency the assurance of my high consideration.

(Signed) F. DAINESE,
Acting Consul General.

To His Excellency CHERIF PACHA,
Minister for Foreign Affairs at Cairo.

With a view to have some action through the Viceroy, Mr. Dainese went to Cairo, and, after consultation with Mr. Thayer, who was lying ill there, he sought of His Highness an interview, which was promptly granted, as the following letters show:

No. 27.

Mr. Dainese to Teki Bey.

[Translated Copy.]

HOTEL DES AMBASSADEURS,
CAIRO, *24th January*, 1864.

EXCELLENCY: I desire to have the honor of an interview with His Highness the Viceroy. Will you be so obliging as to inform me of the day and hour at which His Highness will receive me.

I beg your Excellency to accept the assurance of my high consideration.

(Signed) F. DAINESE,
Acting U. S. Consul General.

To His Excellency TEKI BEY,
Master of Ceremonies of H. H. the Viceroy.

Teki Bey to Mr. Dainese.

[Translated Copy.]

CAIRO, *24th January*, 1864.

SIR: Agreeable to your desire, His Highness will have the pleasure of receiving you to-morrow, at 2½ in the afternoon, at his Palace of Abden.

Accept, sir, the assurance of my high consideration.

(Signed) TEKI BEY.

F. DAINESE, Esq.,
Acting Consul General of America.

This interview led to additional promises, without tangible results, as the sequel shows; whereupon, and after some additional correspondence and further vain efforts to obtain justice, the protest hereinafter was decided upon.

No. 28.

Mr. Dainese to Cherif Pacha.

[Translated Copy.]

U. S. CONSULATE GENERAL IN EGYPT,
ALEXANDRIA, *January* 30, 1864.

EXCELLENCY: I am in receipt of the despatch of your

Ministry, dated the 27th instant, in answer to only a portion of that which this Agency addressed you on the 26th of October last; and I now have to observe, and beg you to note the fact, that you have been three months in sending the answer in question.

It puts forward the statements, firstly, that the claim of Messrs. George and Thomas Kindineco had been settled with the Austrian Consulate General; secondly, that the Egyptian government can only take into consideration the acts emanating from the said consulate respecting that claim.

As the Messrs. Kindineco deny that any such settlement has ever taken place, and as their assertion appears to be sustained by your own offer to take into consideration their acts in this matter, which would be sent you through an irregular channel, I am under the necessity of requesting you—

1st. To supply me with proof in support of your first proposition.

2d. As Messrs. Kindineco are under American protection, and as this Agency is their duly recognized and the only competent authority for the transmission of their acts and the defence of their affairs, I must also beg you to quote the principle of international right which authorizes or justifies your second proposition.

Allow me further to remark, that if any one under your protection were to apply to our consulate for the transmission of his acts, and demand through it payment by the Egyptian Government of his property and dues, you would pay no more serious attention to the demand than I do to that made by you with reference to Messrs. Kindineco; and I conclude with the declaration that the Egyptian Government ought to receive, consider, and answer, within the customary delays, the acts forwarded to it by this Agency concerning the rights of those who are under its protection; and that it will be impossible for it to refuse this without violating its rights, failing in courtesy to the United States of America, and placing itself under the weight of grave responsibilities, which, I trust, you will avoid by adopting towards this Agency a different line of action to that which you have followed for some time, as is attested by a long list of pending claims.

I seize this opportunity of renewing to your Excellency the assurance of my high consideration.

(Signed) F. DAINESE,
Acting Consul General.

To His Excellency CHERIF PACHA,
Minister for Foreign Affairs.

No. 29.

Mr. Dainese to Cherif Pacha.

[Translated Copy.]

U. S. CONSULATE GENERAL IN EGYPT,
ALEXANDRIA, *February* 8, 1864.

EXCELLENCY: I have just received the circular, No. 57, which you did me the honor of addressing me on the 3d of this month, transmitting a printed paper, entitled "Rules affecting Foreign Consulates," communicated, say you, by the Sublime Porte, and having for object an International Convention applicable to Egypt.

As this printed document is neither preceded nor followed by the usual introductive formalities or signatures, and as it bears no sign whatever of having been approved by the contracting parties—things indispensable to give force of law to a regulation which has for object to change existing treaties—and as also my Government has not advised me of its existence, and its very tenor shows that it neither concerns nor is applicable to Egypt, I can only consider it, Monsieur le Minister, as a project which I shall submit to my Government and await its instructions before using it in our relations, which, in the meanwhile, must continue on their former footing.

Accept, Excellency, the assurance of my high consideration.

(Signed) F. DAINESE,
Acting Consul General.

To his Excellency CHERIF PACHA,
Minister for Foreign Affairs.

No. 30.

Mr. Dainese to Cherif Pacha.

[Translated Copy.]

U. S. CONSULATE GENERAL IN EGYPT,
ALEXANDRIA, *9th February*, 1864.

EXCELLENCY: By a communication dated the 8th of last September, this Agency transmitted you a claim of the late Mr. Diamandidi, and renewed it on the 11th of November following. In two despatches, bearing date the 15th and 17th of September, it also called for the execution of a sentence by arbitration in favor of Mr. Anhuri; in those of the 17th, 21st, and 22d October, it announced to you the appointment of certain consular "employés," begging you to cause their recognition. In that of the 26th, ditto, it called the attention of the Egyptian Government to the claims of Messrs. Anhuri, Kindineco and Wassif el Hayat; in that of November 2d, it demanded reparation for Mr. Abellana for the money which had been taken from him on the railway.

In addition to these demands there exists before the Governor here a claim from Messrs. Gsell and Bircher for stones carried away from their ground by local subjects; another of Mr. F. Tourmbé, for the non-execution on the part of the "Madzlis el Wardat" of a contract adjudged to him; and before the Mahia and Governor of Cairo a claim from Janni Nicola, for the seizure by Government of a piece of ground at Ghizeh, belonging to him; and that of Mr. Jean Cumins, for bales of merchandise lost by the railway officials; together with others of less importance.

Many of these claims date from years back.

Not only has no justice been rendered to the complainants, but your Ministry has even omitted to reply to some of the above-mentioned despatches, whilst it has made with regard to others promises, the fulfillment of which is still waited for, and it opposed to the rest objections having no foundation on right, and which this Agency has been under the necessity of refuting in its notes of the 4th and 14th November, and following, which it now confirms.

In presence of this state of things, this Agency, whilst it insists upon its demands hereabove recited, and whilst fully protesting with ample reserves for all that is protestable, it also declares by these presents, and begs you to note, that it holds the Egyptian Government responsible for all the consequences which have resulted from the line of action it has followed, and for all those which may result by a persistence in the same course.

The undersigned has the honor to renew to your Excellency the assurance of his high consideration.

(Signed) F. DAINESE,
Acting Consul General.

To His Excellency CHERIF PACHA,
Minister for Foreign Affairs.

No. 31.

Mr. Dainese to Cherif Pacha.

[Translated Copy.]

U. S. CONSULATE GENERAL IN EGYPT,
ALEXANDRIA, *February* 15, 1864.

EXCELLENCY: I have the honor to transmit enclosed a request from Mr. Jean Cumins, American protégé, accompanied by an account for piastres 15,800, which he claims from the railway administration, as the cost of five bales of merchandise, for which he holds the receipt, and which they have lost.

As this claim has been already for some time before the Government, without any action, I beg you to order its settlement; and I renew to your Excellency the assurance of my high consideration.

(Signed) F. DAINESE,
Acting Consul General.

To His Excellency CHERIF PACHA,
Minister for Foreign Affairs.

No. 32.

Mr. Dainese to Cherif Pacha.

[Translated Copy.]

U. S. Consulate General in Egypt,
Alexandria, *February* 16, 1864.

Excellency: I have just received the despatch which you have done me the honor of addressing me, under date the 8th of this month, No. 70. It modifies your previous letter of the 27th of last January, and encloses the copy of a letter of Mr. G. Schreiner in support of your assertion that *the claim of Messrs. George and Thomas Kindineco* had been settled.

Communication of this copy will be made to the above mentioned for their explanations, which will be transmitted to you in due course.

As to what concerns the question of right, I must remind you that the second proposition in your despatch of the 27th of January, confuted by my note of the 30th ditto, whilst its wording left it evident that Messrs. Kindineco's claim was still pending, yet it maintained that it ought to be carried on by the channel of the Austrian consulate; whereupon I asked for the quotation of the principle of international right authorizing or justifying such a proposition.

Your despatch of the 8th instant, while eluding this principal question, affirms, in substance, that the affair of the Kindinecos, having been settled through Austrian intervention, could not be recommenced under the American authorities—adding, that the principle on which you took your stand was too simple to be discussed.

As every principle of right rejects the resumption of any cause which has been definitely settled according to law, I am under the necessity of observing that, if your proposition already cited had been to this effect, it would never have been discussed; but I also observe to you that no principle within my knowledge takes away from the claimant who may have changed his nationality the right of claiming his property through the channel of his new authority in a pending cause; neither does any principle authorize the defendant to dictate to the other by what channel he ought to seek his rights; and, as your preceding letter sustained the contrary, I asked, and again ask, on what principle you ground your assertion.

Your above mentioned despatch of the 8th, in answer to my note of the 30th of January, contains the following paragraph:

"Besides this affair, there are others which have been pending *for three months*, and which, to quote your own expression, Mr. Acting Consul General, have received no answer within the customary delays."

A simple reference to my aforesaid note will show your mistake in attributing this sentence to me.

Many of the pending affairs therein referred to date from *several years back*, and many of them, being within the jurisdiction of the tribunals here and at Cairo, do not consequently need the search after information to be had "at sufficiently great distances," in order to insure their settlement.

Your said despatch of the 8th of February contains, more, over, observations and assertions concerning Messrs. Rahmi-Arcache, and Luca, which have excited my surprise. Firstly, those bearing on the nationality of the two first are gratuitous, the one being under American, and the other under French protection, and the pretension advanced concerning the third is equally repugnant to both reason and law, which do not require the furnishing of proof to a negative, or the pointing out of means for obtaining it. Secondly, because even if the two former were, as you assert, "M. le Ministre," "rayas," and the other unknown to you, these would not be valid objections against their employment or my right to use their services. Thirdly, because the printed paper you have transmitted to me with your circular of the 3d of this month, and of which you seem to make use for sustaining your ground is not yet recognized by my Government nor applied to Egypt; and that, were even such to be the case, it could not have retrospective action or affect the prerogatives of this Agency in such cases; and here allow me to observe, that these gentlemen have been employed during last summer, *according to the then established custom and usage*, and that their nominations were transmitted to you in October, 1863.

I believe it to be useless to remind you also that in our interview of the 20th of November last, you assured me that you had ordered the recognition of both of them, and promised to write immediately for the third being recognized, and I can only attribute to forgetfulness or a misapprehension your observations in said despatch on this subject.

Persuaded that you will set aside the unpleasant consequences which cannot fail to arise from any hindrance to the free exercise of the functions of the above-mentioned agents, and confirming my previous letters, I renew to your Excellency the assurance of my high consideration.

(Signed) F. DAINESE,
Acting Consul General.

To His Excellency CHERIF PACHA,
Minister for Foreign Affairs.

No. 33.

Mr. Dainese to Cherif Pacha.

[Translated Copy.]

U. S. CONSULATE GENERAL IN EGYPT,
ALEXANDRIA, *February* 25, 1864.

EXCELLENCY: In continuation of the notes of this Agency, dated October 26th and January 30th, 1864, and that of 16th inst., with regard to the claim of Messrs. George and Thomas Kindinceo, I have the honor to transmit herewith to you their reply, accompanied by a certificate, duly authenticated, from Mr. G. Schreiner, containing the explanations called for in your despatch of the 8th of this month.

It is to be seen, from these papers, that their claim is still in suspense, and I, therefore, beg you, M. le Ministre, to have the kindness to proceed to its settlement without further delay.

I seize this opportunity to renew to your Excellency the assurance of my high consideration,

(Signed) F. DAINESE,
Acting Consul General.

To His Excellency CHERIF PACHA,
Minister for Foreign Affairs.

No. 34.

[Translated copy of the Austrian Consul's certificate, accompanying Mr. Dainese's dispatch of 25th of February, 1864, to Cherif Pacha.]

CAIRO, *November* 25, 1866.

[No. 2546.] IMPERIAL AND ROYAL AUSTRIAN CONSULATE GENERAL IN EGYPT.

At the request of Messrs., the brothers G. and T. Kindineco, the Consulate General of Austria in Egypt certifies that their law-suit against the Egyptian Government has never had a perfect solution.

In virtue of the convention which should have settled this affair, and which was accepted on one side by the Egyptian Government, and on the other, by this Consulate General, a sum of $29,000, besides the other sums granted to the claimants by way of compensation, was made over by the local government to the Bank of Egypt—a creditor of the Messrs. Kindineco. This transfer has never had the effect desired; notwithstanding the repeated efforts of this Consulate General the Egyptian Government has never engaged and obliged the Bank to which the transfer was made to recognize the consequences of right resulting from it. Until the regulation of this transfer, the above-mentioned convention, of which this transfer forms an integral part, cannot be considered as having been executed.

Moreover, the undersigned certifies that the Messrs. Kindineco have constantly refused to give the Egyptian Government a final quittance for all sums demanded in due form of law. His Highness, the late Viceroy, Said Pacha, in order to end this dispute, had promised the brothers Kindineco, by the medium of the undersigned Consul General, a contract for the supply of timber for five years, and on this condition the Messrs. Kindineco declared themselves disposed to give the receipt required. Nevertheless this promise has never been executed.

THE CONSUL GENERAL OF AUSTRIA,

[No. 240.] [L. S.] G. SCHREINER.

True copy of the original certified to by the Imperial and Royal Consulate General of Austria, Alexandria, September 14, 1864.

About two weeks after the protest of the 9th of February, hereinbefore shown, Mr. Thayer wrote to Mr. Dainese the following letter, whereupon he went to Cairo, and after consultation with Mr. Thayer, as to the next steps to be taken for obtaining redress, it was decided, as a common resort in the East, to intimate to the Egyptian Government, that unless we are better treated, we will strike our flag and depart, which was accordingly done, and elicited new assurances, expecting the fulfilment of which, Mr. Thayer died.

No. 35.

Mr. Thayer to Mr. Dainese.

CAIRO, 24*th February*, 1864.

* * * It is about time to begin *siége operations* in our business with the Viceroy; when do you come up? * *

(Signed) W. S. THAYER.

FRANCES DAINESE, ESQ.,
Act'g Cons'l Gen'l of the U. S. of America, Alexandria.

INTERNATIONAL RIGHTS.

No. 36.

Mr. Modinos to Mr. Dainese.

[Translated Copy.]

CONSULATE GENERAL OF GREECE, IN EGYPT,
[No. 1225, 1274.] ALEXANDRIA, 21*st December*, 1863.

SIR: I am informed by the consul of Greece, at Cairo, that about four months ago, Mr. Constantine Mango, merchant of that city, a Greek subject, born at Syra, of parents enjoying Grecian nationality, asked permission from the consulate at Cairo, to abandon his nationality, which that consul declined, for want of authority so to do, and sent the request to the royal government for its decision.

Nevertheless, Mr. Mango applied to and obtained from the consulate general of the United States its protection, with the papers to that effect.

The laws of Greece punish the subject who arbitrarily changes his nationality. It is true that the Greek government does not seem too *severe* in that respect, nor cares to prosecute Greek subjects naturalized in a foreign country; yet it does not, nor can, recognize them as subjects of that country, unless they have resided therein and have obtained its nationality by regular naturalization, in conformity with the laws to that effect.

Consuls have no right, nor are competent to clothe strangers residing in their districts with the nationality of their States. If such power was recognized in them, great disorder would reign in the relations and the service of the consulates of different powers established in the same city.

For these reasons the Greek government cannot recognize as subject or protégé of America, Mr. C. Mango, and, therefore, I hope that you will dismiss him from American protection, and grant it no more to Greek subjects.

I sieze this opportunity to present to you the assurance of my high consideration.

(Signed) A. E. MODINOS,
Act'g Consul General of Greece.

To FRANCIS DAINESE, ESQ.,
Act'g Cons'l Gen'l of the U. S. A., Alexandria, Egypt.

No. 37.

Mr. Dainese to Mr. Mondios.

[Translated Copy.]

U. S. CONSULATE GENERAL, IN EGYPT,
ALEXANDRIA, 12*th January*, 1864.

SIR: I have just received the despatch which you did me the

honor to address to me on the 21st ult., containing the information communicated to you by the Greek consul at Cairo, and declaring, in substance: 1st. That the laws of Greece punish the subject who *arbitrarily* changes his nationality. 2d. That the Greek Government does not recognize, except conditionally, expatriated subjects as subjects of other countries; and 3d. That Consuls have no right to grant protection to strangers, &c. On the basis of which declarations you ask me to dismiss from American protection Mr. Mango, and to abstain from granting it hereafter to Greek subjects.

I will first ask of you the favor to quote the laws under which you make these three declarations; I then beg leave to observe that the Greek laws which you invoke, rule Greece; that in neutral States, such as Egypt is, international law guides our relations, and that under these, all men of *age* and free from *obligations*—and Mr. Mango is of that class—are at liberty to renounce their nationality and adopt another. (Fœlix, Droit International, Privé, 3d edition, book 1, page 55.) And consuls in the Levant have the right to protect strangers within their districts. (Wheaton Int. Law, 6th edition, page 135.)

This right of protection is even recognized and fully exercised by the Greek consulates in Egypt, from the fact of their keeping innumerable strangers under Greek protection.

Moreover, by a glimpse at the very laws of Greece, which you invoked, I see that both the law of May 15, 1835, and that of September 14, 1856, instead of inflicting any punishment on subjects who expatriate themselves, puts no restriction whatever to their expatriation. And I will also submit that, as all relations between government and subject cease to exist after the latter's renunciation of nationality, the former cannot thenceforth dictate his course for securing to himself another protection, which fact disposes of your declaration, to the effect that the government of Greece cannot recognize the foreign protection granted to a Greek until after he has been naturalized, &c.

Mr. Mango being an associate of the New York Rallis, and his trade requiring American protection, it was granted him at his own request, and I see no good reason for withdrawing it from or for denying it to others of Mr. Mango's class. It is upon this principle that this consulate has made no objection to the withdrawal by Messrs. Riso and others, from American protection, and their adoption of that of Greece.

It must be remembered also, that before granting Mr. Mango's application for protection, I communicated the fact to Mr. Consul General Charalambi, in your presence, with inquiry as to whether he had any legal objection, to which he answered negatively, adding that Mr. Mango was at liberty to renounce Greek nationality and take American protection, but observing that if he desired to secure the privilege of returning to his old allegiance, he must *in that case* depart with the Greek government's authorization. If therefore that authorization is needed *only* to secure to Mr. Mango a future privilege, and he relinquishes it, it is his own business; and the case is so clear, that Mr. Charalambi received Mr. Mango's act of renunciation without hesitation, returning to him an authenticated copy thereof, under No. 1,005 of your Consulate's Register, which copy is on file at this office.

As regards your last declaration, to the effect that the Government of Greece would decline to recognize Mr. Mango as our protégé, this would not be regarded as a punishment to that protégé, whom the protecting power will take care to defend, but an interference with the rights of the latter, which, I hope, will not be attempted.

I seize this opportunity to renew to you the assurance of my high consideration.

(Signed) F. DAINESE,
Acting Consul General.

A. E. MODINOS, Esq., *Acting Consul General of Greece, Alexandria, Egypt.*

No. 38.

Mr. Dainese to Mr. Seward.

[No. 50.] U. S. CONSULATE GENERAL,
ALEXANDRIA, *April* 13, 1864.

SIR: I have to report the painful tidings of the death of W. S. Thayer, Esq., United States consul general for Egypt, which took place on the 10th instant, at his residence here.

Mr. Thayer had long been affected by disease of the lungs, which year after year impaired his health. In July, 1863, he had a severe attack, which was temporarily checked, he not having since then enjoyed good health three days at one time. On Sunday evening, the 3d instant, he complained of a choking sensation. His standing physicians, Drs. Ogilvie and Mackie, were instantly sent for. They attended him till the 7th, when, no change being perceived, I invited two additional members of the medical body, Drs. Warenhorst and Coluci, to consult and act in concert with the former. They agreed upon a system of cure, which was carefully continued, but with no effect. On Saturday night, the 9th instant, he showed some slight improvement, and slept for nearly three hours. He awoke apparently better, but a few minutes later, he stretched and gave up life. Care and solicitude were not spared for his comfort, and if these could lengthen life he would be still among us.

On the afternoon of the 11th instant the funeral ceremonies were solemnized at the consulate general and in the Protestant burying ground of Alexandria, where his remains have been placed. The cortege was attended by the diplomatic and consular corps in uniform, and by a double line of guards, besides the American citizens and protégés of Alexandria, and a very large concourse of European residents, all of whom were in so friendly terms with the deceased as to feel a sense of personal loss in his death. The pall-bearers were the chief representatives of France, Italy, Holland, Sweden, Norway, the acting consul general of Prussia, and the British consul, the chiefs of the two latter being absent.

Mr. Thayer had hardly attained the prime of life when death so untimely carried him away. His eminent social qualities had won him the affection of a large circle of friends. His high literary attainments had made him well known to the literary world, and his numerous contributions to magazines and journals have given him a creditable reputation in literature. He was a graduate of Harvard

College, and the honorary member of several literary associations in America and Europe.

As the deceased was urged by his physicians to sail for Europe, and that availing himself of the latitude kindly given him by you, he had decided to go as soon as his strength would permit, he had requested me to continue (under my former credentials, which he never revoked) in managing the consulate general, which I did. I now hold it and its property, subject to the orders of the Department, and will by this very mail write to the family of the deceased respecting his property, for which the steps required by law have already been taken by me.

I am, sir, respectfully, your obedient servant,

F. DAINESE,
Acting Consul General.

Hon. W. H. SEWARD,
Secretary of State.

VIOLATION OF DOMICIL AND REPORT OF HALE'S CONDUCT IN EGYPT.

No. 39.

Mr Dainese to Mr. Lincoln.

To His Excellency the President of the United States:

MR. PRESIDENT: A few days since, whilst on my return from the mineral baths, where I had sought to cure the severe illness I had contracted in Alexandria, I read Mr. Hale's published address to the Viceroy of Egypt (of which a translated copy herewith) wherein, in your name, he censures the course adopted by me as Acting Consul General, whilst at the same time, he eulogises Mr. Thayer's line of action.

The sordid motives which are said to have dictated Mr. Hale's conduct in the affair of the flag, necessitated that for appearance sake, and in order to coax the Viceroy, he should put forward as an excuse for reversing my measures, some imaginary wrong on our part, and, in order to effect this, he has not scrupled, having a wholesome fear of Mr. Thayer's friends before his eyes, to make me serve as scapegoat in the address in question.

But your well known sense of justice sufficiently assures me that the expressions used in that document were unauthorized by you, or, that, if authorized, the authority to use them has been obtained by erroneous statements with reference to facts and occurrences which I now submit to you from my point of view—a glance at which will demonstrate. 1st, that my course from the beginning of my charge was simply that initiated and directed by Mr. Thayer; 2d, that it was indispensable *in an eastern country*, and more consistent with our national dignity than Mr. Hale's; and 3d, that his censure of it involves a condemnation of Mr. Thayer's conduct, and causes the United States to appear insensible to the last insult offered to that gentleman's remains, as stated hereafter.

In the summer of 1863, at the pressing solicitation of Mr. Thayer, I consented to take charge of and conduct the United States Consulate General at Alexandria until his return. He apprised the Department of State of this in despatch No. 38 (herewith in copy), and the local authorities and foreign representatives by circulars and letters marked A, B. In presenting me to the Viceroy, he demanded in the name of our Government, and was promised, the immediate settlement through me of all the old pending claims.

After Mr. Thayer's departure, I obtained and sent to London to Mr. Adams, our minister, the evidence necessary to insure the seizure at Birkenhead of two hostile rams, and of this I informed the State Department in despatches No. 39, 41.

Subsequently I carried to our advantage, a point of international law touching a question of jurisdiction between the American and British authorities in Egypt, and adjusted satisfactorily the difficulty involved, as was stated to the Department in despatches No. 40 and 42.

Later, I had to assume charge of and conduct, at my own

expense, and with an increase of labor, the United States vice-consulate at Cairo, whilst, at the same time, I attended to the business at Alexandria and the unsettled claims left in my charge; and, after Mr. Thayer's return and Mr. Vice Consul March's arrival and death, it fell to me to arrange the complicated affairs of the latter, and settle his estâte.

Mr. Thayer approved of and thanked me for all I had done, and begged me to continue to act and aid him, a request to which I only acceded from regard to his delicate health.

As the old claims still remained unsettled, Mr. Thayer duly complained thereof through me, and as our representations produced no tangible result, directed and dictated the protest of February 9th, 1864, (herewith in copy,) and marked C, to be made.

This protest also, being productive of no good effect, we intimated to the authorities that a continuance of such ill treatment would compel us to strike our flag and leave. This elicited excuses and renewed promises that justice should be done, and whilst he awaited their fulfilment death overtook him.

On this melancholy occasion the authorities displayed unmistakeably their "animus" by omitting the customary attendance at his funeral—a lack of respect noticed by the whole consular body and denounced by the local press. A demand for an explanation of this want of courtesy and common feeling remained entirely unanswered.

After Mr. Thayer's death it was my evident duty to continue to conduct his official affairs until such time as the Department, duly apprized by me of the event in despatch No. 50, should provide a successor to the deceased. I followed up his plans and again met with renewed promises until the 15th of July, when the police, in defiance of consular jurisdiction, deliberately violated an American domicile (that of Mr. Thomas Kindineco), beating its owner, and for this I demanded reparation, which being refused, both the national honor, and the action of our own and foreign representatives in like cases, Mr. Consul Macauley's precedent in

1852 approved of by Mr. Webster, and the line of conduct previously adopted by Mr. Thayer, seemed to make it my imperative duty to insist upon redress, with the declaration that, in the event of refusal I should be under the necessity of striking my flag and suspending diplomatic relations.

In the course of the previous year, Mr. Acting Consul General De Beauval had, in view of a minor affair, demanded and obtained the reparation he sought, and as that which I required was not given at the time specified, I acted in accordance with my declaration.

Soon after this, His Highness the Viceroy, entrusted Mr. Tastio, Agent and Consul General of France, with the mission of effecting some arrangement, and after a few days' negotiation, a reparation accompanied by guarantees for the settlement of all claims pending, was promised through that gentleman; we were thus on the point of bringing the matter to a satisfactory and triumphant termination, when the reported unpatriotic interference of an old foe, temporarily in charge of the legation at Constantinople, arrested further proceedings, and Mr. Hale's subsequent conduct entirely put an end to what would otherwise have proved an assured success.

This conduct, and Mr. Hale's antecedents in Egypt in 1862, are more particularly described in my despatch, No. 57, herewith in copy, with its accompaniments wherein he is accused by affidavits, of having acted in consequence of the receipt of large presents; I also add for reference copies of my other despatches No. 54 to 59 to the Department, together with as many of their enclosures as escaped his clutches, in illustration of the whole transaction. They are substantially correct copies of the originals, although owing to their having been copied from rough drafts, there may be some slight changes in their wording.

It should be remembered, Mr. President, that although ever ready to serve my country (witness the services I rendered at home at the commencement of our national difficulties, and particularly on the night of the 26th of April, 1861, when I received the distinguished honor of your personal thanks), and disposed to exert myself for the common welfare, *I never asked or solicited* the charge of Acting Consul General in Egypt, which was, in some sort, forced on and only accepted by me for a time in order to relieve Mr. Thayer, whose ill health required repose and change of scene.

I never either demanded or received any pecuniary emolument for the task I undertook.

After Mr. Thayer's death, which I duly announced to the Department, five months elapsed before I was relieved from my duties, and during all that period I devoted my fullest attention and labor to the extensive pending business of the consulate general; although, in order to do so, I was compelled to neglect my own private affairs, which have, consequently, suffered considerably, and I have never even been reimbursed in my official expenses.

Whilst in charge of the office, I comported myself to the best of my judgment and ability, for the honor of our country and for the amelioration of the interest of our citizens and "protégés" in Egypt; and the course I adopted and the services I rendered did not fail to elicit the approval and praise of distinguished Americans, of the Christian community, and those we protected. In fact, in testimony of their satisfaction, they recently sent me a very kind letter, herewith in copy, marked D, accompanied by a gift of over six thousand dollars, (in that time's value of currency,) which I forwarded home for the relief of our suffering brethren, and which, as concerns its liberality, is, as yet, unequalled by the contributions forwarded by other consuls.* (See despatch No. 53.)

Committee of Protégés to Mr. Dainese.

ALEXANDRIA, *6th of July*, 1864.

F. DAINESE, Esq., *Acting U. S. Consul General for Egypt.*

SIR: Feeling deeply the calamities of war in the United States, under whose powerful protection we are living in Egypt, and being desirous of showing, both to yourself, sir, and to the American people and government, our full appreciation of that protection, and our sympathy for the sufferings of our struggling brethren, we herewith enclose a purse, containing five hundred and seventy-seven pounds sterling and four shillings, accompanied by a list of subscri-

If that course and those services, proceeding, as they did, from a consciousness of right and the dictates of an honest

---

bers, which, as a committee selected amongst them, we request you in their names to accept as our contribution for the relief of the widows and orphans of those who have fallen victims in defending the Union.

We are, sir, respectfully, your most obedient servants,

(Signed) A. M. RALLI,
T. STIER,
CONSTANTINE G. MANGO,
SOLIMAN EFFENDI RAHMI.

Names of the Subscribers.	*Amount in Pounds Sterling.*
A. M. Ralli	£150
T. G. Rodocanachi & Sons	60
Soliman Effendi Rahmi	50
Aïoub Babazogli	50
C. G. Mango	30
T. Stier	20
G. N. Kindineco	20
Thomas N. Kindineco	20
F. Cordachi	20
B. Coury	20
A. Sambreau	20
Y. Barthow	10
D. G. Mizevere	10
J. S. Miriango	10
S. S. Constantino	10
Giuseppe Auad	10
Habib Arcache	10
Alessandro K. Kampani	10
Napoleone Galli	10
Nissa Bircher	10
Ibrahim Mileka	5
Abdalla Tamburgi	5
G. Oskar	5
Salek Avat	4
S. Milner	4
A. Cumin	3 4
G. Telatinidi	1
	£577 4s

Mr. Chase to Mr. Dainese.

(Copy.)

CHERRY HILL, NEAR SALEM, MASS., *Aug.* 26, 1864.

DEAR MR. DAINESE: Your note reached me at this place, where I have been spending a few days since I have retired from office. I was much gratified by the proof it brought, not only of your own zeal for the Union, but of the interest inspired by you to others.

I have already commended your letter to Mr. Fessenden, my successor, who will be as much gratified by it as I am, and will also soon comply with your wish concerning the publication of the letter and names.

With best wishes, yours truly,

(Signed) S. P. CHASE.

F. DAINESE, Esq.

heart, fail to be approved of at home, they will not, I am sure, be considered deserving of censure, and will, I hope, be freed from your disapproval by a removal of the expressions, as I believe, surreptitiously used in your name by Mr. Hale, in his address mentioned at the commencement of this letter.

The wrongs I have here noticed and explained in despatches Nos. 57, 58, and 59, are of two classes: first, those which involve the dignity of the Government, and in bringing which to your notice I have only fulfilled my duty as a citizen; and secondly, those which immediately injure my private interests, and for which I hope to obtain early redress at your hands.

I have the honor to be, with the highest respect, Mr. President, your most obedient servant,

(Signed) F. DAINESE.

GENEVA, *December* 18, 1864.

No. 40.

Hale's Address to the Viceroy.

(Translation of the address presented to His Highness the Viceroy of Egypt by the Agent and Consul General of the United States of America, on the 30th of October, 1864. Extract from the "*Spettatore Egiziano.*")

HIGHNESS: The President of the United States of America has made himself acquainted with my report concerning the events which occurred in Egypt before my arrival, and after the decease of my predecessor.

I am directed by the President to assure your Highness that he has learnt with much regret that, after the irreparable loss of Mr. Thayer, his eminent and cherished representative near your Highness, unsuitable measures had been adopted *by an accidental consul general.**

* Mr. Dainese thinks that he was not any less the rightful incumbent of the Consulate General in Egypt than President Johnson is that of the White House. The deaths of the rightful appointees compelled both to assume their duties. The Constitution provides for the emergency in the case of the President. The diplomatic and consular regulations approved and followed by the whole civilized world provide for that in the case of Mr. Dainese.

Above all, the consular flag having been struck without either the general or private authorization of the American Government, this very regretable act is specially disavowed.

I am instructed to refuse all protection to Kindineco and Santi, who have been the cause of the last embarrassments.

Lastly, I am directed to assure your Highness that the President has ever been, and still is, desirous of cultivating the sincerest relations of friendship with your Highness's Government.

Remarks on the foregoing Document.

The "accidental consul" can be no other than Mr. Dainese, who, notwithstanding this artful attempt to discredit him, was, and had never ceased to be, to all intents and purposes, after his nomination by Mr. Thayer, the accredited Agent and Acting Consul General of the United States at Alexandria, during Mr. Thayer's absence, and was so recognized by all the authorities and the diplomatic and consular body in Egypt.

Mr. Dainese was and is under the impression that, as the representative of Mr. Thayer and, through him, of the United States Government, he was fully justified in taking such measures for the redress of the insult offered the consulate, and the further grasp of American interests, as Mr. Thayer, whose delegate he was, would have adopted had he been personally present, as is testified by the protest of February, 1864, written to his dictation, against the multifarious misdeeds of the Egyptian authorities.

The term "regretable," (facheux,) applied by Mr. Hale to Mr. Dainese's line of action, can hardly be applicable, unless it be admitted that, notwithstanding many grievous wrongs, the American Government has decided to avoid any discussion with foreign powers, even at the expense of justice and the national dignity of this country—and this Mr. Dainese cannot believe to be the case.

To disavow his proceedings will, he boldly asserts, only lead to further complications, owing to the tortuous character of Oriental politicians; and Mr. Hale, who has sought to win favor with the magnates of Egypt by withdrawing all protection from Messrs. Kindineco and Santi, and abandoning them to their oppressors, will, in future, be compelled to adhere to the same degrading and subservient policy, and become a cipher for any good purpose, as far as our national interests in Egypt are concerned.

No. 41.

Mr. Dainese to Mr. Seward.

[No. 54.] U. S. CONSULATE GENERAL,
ALEXANDRIA, *July* 21, 1864.

SIR: I have the honor to report that on the 15th inst. an American domicile was brutally violated by some forty armed policemen, headed by a deputy of the chief of police; its owner was beaten and dragged forth from his place, and his men who were engaged in the erection of a small Perry pump, driven by horse-power, imprisoned, and the work stopped.

Before this, the chief of the police, in a note dated the 13th inst., requested this consulate to stop the work, *because a steam engine was being erected, and could not be without special permission.*

Promptly, according to the request, this consulate caused the work to be stayed until, after the examination, it was ascertained that there was no *steam engine* on the premises, and that the reason assigned by the police did not exist; it, therefore, removed the injunction, at the same time apprizing the police of its reasons for so doing.

It was not until after this that the police, at 6 A. M. of the 15th inst., perpetrated the act before mentioned, and at 9 A. M., *three hours after*, I received a note from its chief, bearing date the 14th, intimating his intention of acting as he did. This latter step can only be regarded as a direct and intentional insult to the consulate.

Under my credentials from the late Mr. Thayer, as "Acting U. S. Consul General," and recognized and addressed as such by this government, and by the consulates of foreign powers, there remained to me but one alternative under the circumstances, namely, to demand the immediate arrest and punishment of the offenders; any other course would, in the eyes of these people, appear an omission to resent, on the part of the United States, one of the grossest insults ever offered to a foreign power, and in this my opinion, my colleagues, the English, French, and Italian Consuls General, cordially concurred.

The satisfaction thus demanded being declined, owing to certain intrigues, I telegraphed to the Viceroy that if it was not given by the 20th inst. at noon, I should haul down the United States flag and suspend diplomatic relations with his government. His Highness being exclusively occupied with matters of trade, and having abandoned affairs of State to his ministers, referred the business to them. They held a council in which the wisest urged that my demand be acceded to, seeing that right was on my side, and that sooner or later concessions must necessarily be made; others, led by Cherif Pacha, Minister for Foreign Affairs, and a bitter enemy of the United States, opposed the proposition on the ground "that Americans might be bullied now because they were busy at home, and had no vessels disposable to hurt Egypt."

Meanwhile the time allowed for satisfaction expired before any had been offered, and, at the appointed hour, I hauled down our flag.

I am well aware that these tidings will be unwelcome to the Department; but my duty to my country and my regard for its dignity required, I opine, that I should adopt this and no other course. The sanctity of a domicil was scrupulously respected even in the remotest and most barbarous periods of Turkish history; and if its violation be once permitted, our citizens in Egypt will daily be exposed to searches and plunder, and our missionaries, in particular, will be the first to suffer.

Not long ago a French subject was beaten by the military. The French consul demanded the degradation of the offending officer and the punishment of the soldiers concerned. The Viceroy hesitated, and the consul then threatened to haul down his flag if satisfaction were not instantly given. This demand was granted at once. The presence of two French men-of-war in the harbor had a magical effect on this occasion. The arrival of ours, or the slightest show of determination on our part, undoubtedly will bring about the same result.

I enclose copy of my despatch on the subject addressed to our naval officers, and hope that it will receive the approval of the Department.

I am, sir, respectfully, your obedient servant,

(Signed) F. DAINESE,

Acting U. S. Consul General.

To Honorable W. H. SEWARD,

Secretary of State.

No. 42.

Mr. Dainese to Mr. Seward.

[No. 55.] U. S. CONSULATE GENERAL,
ALEXANDRIA, *4th August*, 1864.

SIR: On the 21st ultimo, by despatch No. 54, I had the honor to inform the Department of the hauling down of the United States flag, in consequence of the refusal of the Egyptian Government to give satisfaction for the violation of an American domicil, and for the insult offered to this consulate.

On the 2d instant, His Highness the Viceroy, after his return to town, despatched to me, Mr. Tastu, agent and Consul General of France, to make overtures of arrangement. I manifested my readiness to accept any proposal consistent with the honor of the United States, and proceeded then, with Mr. Tastu, to review the matter.

Mr. Tastu, in the Viceroy's name, proposed that we should rehoist our flag, under a salute of 21 guns, and that after this he should investigate the case, and give the satisfaction required. I, however, was under the necessity of declining to accede to this offer, because the violation of an American domicil, and insult to our flag, were so flagrant and obvious that, in my humble opinion, satisfaction should be rendered before the flag could again be raised.

His Highness, according to Mr. Tastu's report, found fault with my not having awaited his return, previous to hauling down the flag, or informing him of my intention of doing so, "as he would have done me justice." I exhibited the receipt from the telegraph office, showing, beyond doubt, that His Highness received my despatch to that effect, three days before the hauling down of the flag; said that he made neither reply to it, nor asked me to wait, and requested Mr. Tastu to remind him that a demand in writing, for explanation with reference to the want of respect shown the United States, by his ministers, in not paying Mr. Thayer due honors last April, still remained unnoticed. I added that the last event,* although in itself sufficient to justify the course I had pursued, was simply the drop which caused the overflowing of the cup of injustices inflicted on American interests, and of the disregard of our consular rights, exhibited by His Highness's ministers during the last past ten months; and I observed that in the course of last February, we had been compelled to protest most formally against the Egyptian government for all these short comings. I also gave Mr. Tastu a memorandum of our grievances, which he undertook to present to His Highness.

Yesterday Mr. Tastu came again with a promise from His Highness to settle, immediately, all pending claims, in consideration of my yielding the point of satisfaction, previous to the rehoisting of our flag, and assurances were given and guarantees through Mr. Tastu that full satisfaction would ensue. I insist upon having it beforehand, and am sanguine of obtaining it, as most of the ministers of this government evince considerable uneasiness at the existence of any difficulty with America.

I am, sir, very respectfully, your obedient servant,

(Signed) F. DAINESE,

Acting Consul General.

Hon. W. H. SEWARD,

Secretary of State.

No. 13.

Mr. Dainese to Mr. Seward.

[No. 56.] U. S. CONSULATE GENERAL,

ALEXANDRIA, *August 12th*, 1864.

SIR: In continuation of my dispatch of the 4th inst., No. 55, I have to inform the Department that Mr. Tastu, the agent and Consul General of France, chosen by His Highness the Viceroy to arrange our difficulty with the Egyptian government, reports to me that, after deciding on a plan of accommodation in accord-

* The violation of domicil.

ance with my memorandum, which appeared to be satisfactory and to the honor of both parties, when he applied for the Viceroy's order for its fulfillment, he was told that a letter had just been received from the Turkish Minister for Foreign Affairs, inviting the Viceroy, at the request of Mr. John P. Brown, acting U. S. "Chargé d'Affairs," at Constantinople, not to settle the dispute with me, because (Dainese) was not recognized by an "exequatur" from the "Porte," obtained through our "Constantinople Legation," and bidding him to have no uneasiness on the subject, inasmuch as he (Mr. Brown,) "would write to Washington and settle it." This caused a cessation of all further negotiations, and Mr. Tastu indignant at the pursual of such a course on the part of the person acting as our "Chargé d'Affairs," observed to the Viceroy that it was now too late to refuse to recognize me in the settlement of this affair, when he had already recognized and corresponded with me up to the day of its occurrence; nevertheless, His Highness decided to act on Mr. Brown's suggestions.

Leaving to the Department the appreciation of such conduct on the part of our acting "Chargé d'Affairs," I respectfully request that he be called to account therefor; I claim to have acted in strict accordance with the exigencies of circumstances, and as the honor of the American nation required, and to have brought the Egyptian government to the verge of affording us full satisfaction, and of settling all claims due to Americans, and I accuse Mr. J. P. Brown of having, by his uncalled for and unnecessary interference, and insinuations, prevented my success at the very moment it was on the point of attainment, and to this the French Consul General will bear witness.

Herewith, I enclose copies of correspondence concerning this and previous difficulties with this Government, and a memorandum of the arrangement proposed, and have the honor to be, sir, respectfully,

Your obedient servant,

(Signed) F. DAINESE,

Acting Consul General.

HON. W. H. SEWARD,

Secretary of State.

No. 44.

Police Department to Mr. Dainese.

[Translated Copy.]

[No. 11, 123.] ALEXANDRIA, 8 *Saper*, 1281, *Hegira*,
13 *July*, 1864.

TO THE ACT. CONSUL-GENERAL OF THE U. S. OF AMERICA:

In consequence of a letter received from the muhaven of the 5th and 6th district, informing me of the placing by Mr. Thomas Kindineco of iron machines and of a mill at the mouth of a cistern belonging to the government, I wrote to the "ornato" * on the subject, who sent to verify the fact.

I now am in receipt of this answer, No. 24, to the effect that the engineers of the ornato and of the "intendance" of the fortifications have stated that the placing of steam engines has caused the rupture of the mouth of a cistern, and that the placing of machines on the said cistern is prohibited by superior authority, and that it is urgent that they should be removed, and that the cistern should be closed as it had been previously.

Consequently, as the placing of such machines is prohibited, unless by permission of the civil authorities, I address you the present letter, of which the bearers are Mr. B. Prosper and the above-mentioned muhaven, in the hope that some one may be named and sent on the part of the consulate to stop the works conducted by Mr. Kindineco, and to enjoin him to do nothing further until he has obtained the necessary permission from the local authorities, according to custom.

(Signed) THE ADJUTANT OF POLICE,
Of Alexandria.

[Seal of the Police.]

No. 45.

Mr. Dainese to Khourshoud Pacha.

[Translated Copy.]

U. S. CONSULATE GENERAL IN EGYPT,
ALEXANDRIA, *July* 14, 1864.

EXCELLENCY: In consequence of a report from the engineers of the local government, sent to me through your muha-

* The ornato is the corps of engineers.

ven (deputy), and according to which, Mr. Kindineco had placed a steam engine on his grounds without having previously obtained the permission of the local authorities, I have, in conformity with your request, caused the works undertaken by the said Mr. Kindineco, to be suspended since yesterday.

Now, however, that I have examined the affair in question, I find that Mr. Kindineco has set up no sort of steam engine, but simply a pump with horse-power for trial; consequently the report of the Government engineers, on the strength of which, I, at your request, caused the works to be suspended, is inexact. I have, therefore, just permitted Mr. Kindineco to resume his work, and I trust that the government engineers who have sought to obstruct it will be reprimanded, so as to prevent any repetition of similar acts on their part in future.

Receive the assurance, &c., &c.,

(Signed) F. DAINESE,
Acting Consul-General.

His Excellency KHOURSHOUD PACHA,
Minister of Police, Alexandria.

No. 46.

Khourshoud Pacha to Mr. Dainese.

[Translated Copy.]

[No. 72, 162.] POLICE DEPARTMENT, ALEXANDRIA,
9 *Safer*, 1281, *Hegira*, (14*th July*, 1864.)

I have made myself acquainted with the letter from your consulate, in which it is said that the works of Mr. Kindineco have not been suspended because the engineers were in error in asserting that he had a steam engine there.

Even were it to be admitted that the iron machines which are down there were the instruments, (sii,) belonging to a steam engine, to a pump, or no matter what else, I reply to you that all works of this description are forbidden, unless authorized, particularly when wells and cisterns, the property of the government, and where mouths have been opened, are concerned.

In consequence, I write you this present letter, and hope that you will invite the above-mentioned Mr. Kindineco to suspend works which he is not authorized to carry on by the local government. I have also written to the proper parties to see to the execution of my orders.

(Signed) MAHMOUD KHOURSHOUD,
Prefect of Police.

Mr. DAINESE,
U. S. Acting Consul General, Alexandria.

No. 47.

Mr. Dainese to Cherif Pacha.

[Translated Copy.]

CONSULATE GENERAL OF THE U. S. OF AMERICA,
ALEXANDRIA, *July* 15, 1864.

EXCELLENCY: The American domicil of Mr. Thomas Kindineco has been violated this morning by men of the local police, with the muhaven at their head. His people, engaged on a certain work, were dragged to prison, and himself arrested, beaten, and maltreated, as you will see by the document hereunto annexed.

These acts of brutality inaugurated by the police being revolting and in flagrant violation of treaties, I demand, as the representative of the American Government, the immediate arrest of the muhaven and of the other perpetrators thereof, and their punishment, together with that of those by whose orders they have acted; and, in the meanwhile, I protest against the Egyptian government, with all the usual reserves and formalities in like cases. I renew to your Excellency the assurance of my high consideration.

(Signed) F. DAINESE,
Acting Consul General.

To His Excellency CHERIF PACHA, *Minister for Foreign Affairs to His Highness the Viceroy, Alexandria.*

No. 48.

Cherif Pacha to Mr. Dainese.

[No. 569.] MINISTRY OF FOREIGN AFFAIRS,
ALEXANDRIA, *July* 16, 1864.

SIR: I have received the despatch you did me the honor of addressing me on the 15th instant, with Mr. Kindineco's complaint against the police of Alexandria, and an exposition of the reasons on which it is based.

I immediately wrote to the police of Alexandria to send, without delay, to me precise explanations on this subject; and, as soon as I shall have received them, I will lose no time in making such reparation to the above-mentioned as he may be entitled to.

Pray accept, sir, the assurance of my high consideration.

CHERIF PACHA,
The Minister for Foreign Affairs.

Mr. DAINESE,
Acting Consul General of the U. S. of America.

The above, though dated the 16th, was left at the consulate general by a government messenger on the 18th July, after ample time for consultation with the minister of police had elapsed, and fully shows a disposition to ignore the wrong, and quibble; wherefore the following notices were sent to both His Highness the Viceroy and his minister for foreign affairs:

No. 49.

Mr. Dainese to Cherif Pacha.

[Translated Copy.]

U. S. CONSULATE GENERAL IN EGYPT,
ALEXANDRIA, *July* 18, 1864.

EXCELLENCY: I have just received your despatch, No. 569, dated the 16th instant, which in no wise answers my demand for immediate reparation in consequence of the violation, by order of the local authorities, of an American domicil, and the insults and bad treatment inflicted on the person of its proprietor, Mr. Thomas Kindineco.

I find myself, therefore, under the painful necessity of

declaring to you, that if, on Wednesday, the 20th instant, at noon, full reparation be not granted me, the national flag will be struck, and the diplomatic relations of this Agency with the Egyptian Government suspended.

I have the honor to renew to your Excellency the assurance of my high consideration.

(Signed) F. DAINESE,
Acting Consul General.

To His Excellency CHERIF PACHA,
Minister for Foreign Affairs.

No. 50.

Mr. Dainese to His Highness the Viceroy.

[By Telegraph.—Translated Copy.]

AGENCY AND CONSULATE GENERAL OF THE
UNITED STATES OF AMERICA,
ALEXANDRIA, *July* 18, 1864.

TO HIS HIGHNESS THE VICEROY OF EGYPT, *Mansurah:*

An American domicil having been brutally violated on Friday morning by order of the local authorities, and its owner insulted, beaten, and dragged out of his place, I have demanded immediate reparation; but Cherif Pacha has as yet done nothing. My duty to America forces me to strike the national flag and to suspend my diplomatic relations with your Government, unless, between this and next Wednesday, at noon, full reparation be granted me.

(Signed) F. DAINESE,
Acting Consul General.

No. 51.

Cherif Pacha to Mr. Dainese.

[Translated Copy.]

[No. 590.] MINISTRY OF FOREIGN AFFAIRS,
ALEXANDRIA, *July* 19, 1864.

SIR: I have received the despatch you did me the honor

of writing me, the 18th instant, to inform me that if the immediate reparation demanded in your preceding letter of the 16th of this month, for Mr. Kindineco, were not granted from this to the 20th instant, the American flag would be struck, and the diplomatic relations of the Agency with the Egyptian Government suspended.

The Government of His Highness, the Viceroy, has nothing so much at heart as to preserve the best relations with that which you represent, and it therefore feels much regret for the determination expressed by you.

Always ready to do justice to everybody, it would have made it its duty to satisfy your demands had circumstances permitted it to do so.

But I must be permitted to remark, that in no country whatever can a man be judged and condemned without being heard, and that reparation can only be demanded when, after a regular verification of facts, it is ascertained to be really and legitimately due.

Either at law or equity it was impossible for me to act on the unsupported assertions of Mr. Kindineco.

To judge from the very limited information which I have, on my part, been able to gather in the short space of time which has elapsed since your first communication, the acts complained of would seem to have occurred, not at Mr. Kindineco's domicil, in so far as that denomination would imply the idea of a residence, but on an uninclosed piece of land; and the police appears to have interfered, because your protégé had allowed himself, in order to set his machine at work, to demolish an aquednct intended for the use of the public, and had, moreover, answered the observations addressed to him by personal acts of violence.

The agents of the authority would not, then, be altogether in the wrong, as Mr. Kindineco asserts.

But in order to define the situation clearly and arrive at a regular solution, I am ready to take measures for an inquiry into all the points under discussion immediately.

The civil tribunal of Alexandria will be directed to institute this inquiry in the presence of the consular delegate you may designate, and will give its sentence with reference to the penalties, as laid down by the local laws, incurred by those agents of the authority who may be found guilty.

Such is, in my eyes, the only practicable mode conformable with justice.

Accept, sir, the assurance of my high consideration.

CHERIF PACHA,
Minister for Foreign Affairs.

F. Dainese, Esq., *U. S. Acting Consul General, at Alexandria.*

No. 52.

Mr. Dainese to Cherif Pacha.

[Translated Copy.]

U. S. Consulate General in Egypt,
Alexandria, *July 19th*, 1864.

Excellency: I hasten to reply to your dispatch of to-day, which I have just received.

It appears from its contents that your Ministry has not been well informed with reference to the facts which led me to demand from you immediate reparation for the violation of an American domicil. The facts are these: under date of the 7th of "Safer," the prefect of police addressed me a note informing me that Mr Thomas Kindineco was taking the liberty of erecting a steam-engine on his ground, without having previously obtained the permission of the local authorities.

Being aware of the Government regulations in this respect, and believing in the correctness of what had been said to me, I immediately caused the suspension of the works undertaken by Mr. Kindineco; but on the following day, having verified that it was not a steam-engine, but merely a small horse-power pump which he was erecting on trial, I replied on the same day, the 15th, to the prefect of police, informing him that the report received by him from these engineers was incorrect, and that I had permitted Mr. Kindineco to continue his works.

It is after a declaration of this kind from this Agency, that the local police assumed the right of taking the violent measures complained of, although in the two notes addressed to me by them, and copies of which I enclose, they had acknowledged that the place in question was an American domicil, and that my intervention was necessary for the suspension of the works therein.

Therefore, there is in this act of the police, not only the violation of a domicil, but also the want of respect due to this Agency; and I, on this account, adhere firmly to the terms of my note of the 18th inst., although always prepared, so soon as satisfaction shall have been rendered, to proceed to any inquiry which may be judged proper concerning the matters in dispute between the Government and Mr. Kindineco.

I seize this opportunity to renew to your Excellency the assurance of my high consideration.

(Signed) F. DAINESE,
Acting Consul General.

To His Excellency CHERIF PACHA,
Minister for Foreign Affairs to H. H. the Viceroy,
Alexaudria.

No. 53.

Cherif Pacha to Mr. Dainese.

[Translated Copy.]

[No. 598.] MINISTRY OF FOREIGN AFFAIRS,
ALEXANDRIA, *July 20th*, 1864.

SIR: I hasten to reply to the despatch of yesterday's date, which you did me the honor of addressing me.

It is possible that the department of police should have mistaken the nature of the machine employed by Mr. Kindineco, but it was not on this point that the question depended. Mr. Kindineco's ground is legally bound for the passage of an aqueduct, which contributes to the supply of water in the city, and he has taken the liberty to damage it, and to turn aside its water for his own benefit—that is to say, for the machine he was erecting. It is only then with the view of hindering the continuance of this abuse that, in the interest of the public, the local police has believed it to be its duty urgently to intervene in the matter.

As to the violation of an American domicil, which has been, say you, the consequence of this intervention, permit me to observe to you, that by the word domicil is generally understood the place of residence or habitation of a citizen, and that a simple piece of ground cannot possibly be looked upon in that light.

In what concerns the inquiry of which you accept the principle, whilst, at the same time you wish it to be preceded by reparation, allow me again to remark here that, the signification of these two words, "inquiry" and "reparation," of itself, shows clearly that the first should precede the second, according to every rule of justice.

Might it not, in fact, happen that the inquiry would establish that the person who had already received reparation, was the real culprit, or, at least, the party who had given provocation; in such a case, what would have to be done?

I again appeal to your impartiality, and I trust that, on reflection, you will consent to adopt the course I had the honor of proposing to you, by withdrawing the expressions of an ultimatum not sufficiently justified by facts, and which would cause in so regretable a manner the interruption of the satisfactory relations which have hitherto never ceased to exist between the Egyptian government and the Republic of the United States of America.

Pray accept, sir, the renewed assurance of my sentiments of high consideration.

(Signed) CHERIF PACHA,
Minister for Foreign Affairs.

F. DAINESE, Esq., *Acting Consul General of the U. S. of America, at Alexandria.*

N. B.—This letter was delivered at 12½ P. M., namely, half an hour after the flag was hauled down; Mr. Schwab, one of Cherif Pacha's secretaries, delivered it in the presence of Messrs. Barthow and Tawill, and took memorandum that it was 12½ P. M., and after the flag was down.

No. 54.

Remarks on the foregoing letters of the Alexandria police, dated 8 *and* 9 *Safer, H.* (13*th and* 14*th July*, 1864,) *and of the Egyptian Ministry for Foreign Affairs, of the* 19*th and* 20*th same month*, (*Nos.* 590 *and* 598.)

The allegation that Mr. Kindineco had caused the rupture of a cistern belonging to Government, by opening it, in order to establish a steam-engine and a mill over it, is incorrect.

The ground on which the present city of Alexandria stands is intersected by underground canals, built in the remotest times, some say as far back as the foundation by Alexander, at all events, in the time of the Romans; for, although, as everybody knows, the Turks have systematically damaged all monuments of antiquity, they have done little to repair or keep them in order. These channels receive their water from the Nile, and empty themselves into the sea. They have openings or vents in almost every house or garden, the owners of which have full right to use the water they supply. One of these canals commences beneath Nubar Pacha's property, passing under some two hundred other houses and gardens, *and ending under that belonging to Kindineco*, whence it runs into the sea. At one of its openings, Nubar Pacha has a six-horse-power steam pump for irrigation. The two hundred houses and gardens above alluded to, obtain their supply from similar openings on the grounds appertaining to them, and one of these is on Mr. Kindineco's land; it is on this spot that that gentleman placed a small Perry pump, moved by a Sandford horse-power, for for the sake of experiment. Neither steam-engine nor mill were employed.

The deeds for the land on which the opening exists, convey *the land with all its appurtenances*, to Mr. Kindineco, and do not render it liable to any "servitude," or, as is gratuitously asserted in Cherif Pacha's note of July 20, to the passage of an aqueduct; the portion of the canal or aqueduct which is beneath it is part and parcel of it, and the above-mentioned deeds contain no restrictions or clauses whatever with regard to the use either of the mouth or of the water. Mr. Kindineco has full right to use them, and has hitherto used them after the same fashion as his neighbors Nubar Pacha and the other proprietors have done, with the openings for water on their grounds.

It is, likewise, incorrect that the said land was unenclosed; one hundred and seventy shops were built on its outer front by Mr. Kindineco, who, he informs me, receives from them the annual rent of 180,000 Egyptian piasters; and a gate affords ingress to the centre of these buildings at the spot where Mr. Kindineco was trying his pump; this gate has also been demolished by the Egyptian government, to give passage for a railway.

It is equally contrary to fact that any regulation existed forbidding the erection of a pump by a resident on his own ground; the only ordinance existing at the time of the occurrence, which had been officially communicated and made public, was to the effect that, whenever any proprietor should erect a steam-engine on his own land, he should, before erecting it, notify the government, and obtain permission for so doing.

It is incorrect that Mr Kindineco monopolized the water, and that the police were, on that account, obliged to stop him; it is equally incorrect that he had recourse to violence ("voies de fait";) but even supposing he had done so, he had, when assailed in his own domicil, full right to defend himself on the principle that "every man's house is his castle." In fact, all Cherif Pacha's allegations and reasonings as to the necessity of investigating the matter *before a Mohammedan court* previous to reparation being granted, fall to the ground in the presence of the main question, namely: the fact that Kindineco was erecting something *on his own ground or premises*, and that both *he* and *those premises* were acknowledged by the Egyptian police to *be under American jurisdiction:* and its full knowledge of it is moreover proved by the application in writing of the chief of police to the American consulate for the suspension of the works.

The consulate intervened, stopped the work, examined the matter in dispute, and finding no good reason for complaint, removed its injunction.

The police then, instead of reiterating its recourse through the American consulate, or applying for superior orders from the Viceroy's Government, and make it a case for diplomatic consideration, took the law into its own hands, and in defiance of consular authority broke into the place previously recognized as protected by the American flag, and destroyed the property thereon!

Thus, in addition to the wrong inflicted on an American protégé, a direct insult was offered to our consulate and flag; reparation was demanded and Cherif Pacha, evading the main point, *i. e.*, the insult to the consular authority and its flag, endeavored to make reparation dependant on a trial before *Egyptian courts*, of a matter secondary to the main question.

Now, I maintain that even if, upon examination, Mr. Kindineco had been found to be in the wrong, which is but a supposition, the police were not the less culpable for acting on their own authority on American ground and insulting the consulate, and were not the less deserving of punishment beforehand as demanded by me, more especially as, in my note of July 19th, I left the question of damages claimed by Mr. Kindineco *a secondary matter, to be settled subsequently to the inquiry proposed by Cherif Pacha.*

As regards Cherif Pacha's quibble that "domicil" means the house where one lodges, and that a man's land, shop, or other property can bear no such name, I consider it merely one of his many subterfuges to get out of the scrape.

In Mohammedan countries, where all living under a foreign flag enjoy *exterritoriality*, any place belonging to or occupied by them is their *domicil*, and any trespass thereon constitutes, what is there termed, *a violation of domicil.*

(Signed) F. DAINESE.

No. 55.

Memorandum of arrangement about to be concluded between Mr. Dainese and the Egyptian Government, and which was first arrested by John P. Brown's interference, and finally defeated by Charles Hale's treachery.

1st. The Minister of Police or the French Consul General to call upon the American Consular representative for the purpose of explaining that the police deputy who had violated an American domicil had acted entirely on his own responsibility, and would, therefore, meet with condign punishment.

2d. Simultaneously with this visit, the Minister for Foreign Affairs to address to the American Acting Consul General, a letter expressive of regret for what had passed, and requesting that the United States flag might be re-hoisted under a salute of twenty-one guns, and assuring Mr. Dainese that as an equivalent for the satisfaction demanded, His Highness the Viceroy's Government would settle all pending American claims as detailed hereafter, viz:

Messrs. Soleiman Rahmi, Habib Arcache and Misrale Luka, to be immediately recognized at their respective posts, and that Janni Nicolu likewise receive the sum of one thousand pounds sterling which the late Viceroy, Said Pacha, had promised Mr. Thayer to pay to said Janni for cost and damages of a piece of land forcibly taken from him by the Government agents at Yhizeh; in addition to which Mr. Abellana would receive five hundred and forty piastres unjustly taken from him by the Egyptian railroad agents, and Messrs. Jean Cumins and George Plant would be paid the value of their merchandise lost by the same railroad agents.

In one month to settle the claims of Hanna Hanhuri, against Enani Bey, together with other small matters enumerated in the official correspondence with the foreign office, and the governors of Alexandria and Cairo, and, to settle also within three months, the claims of Messrs. George and Thomas Kindineco, by submitting the same to a tribunal which will decide according to the principles of equity, justice, and common right, and will be composed of two judges nominated by the Egyptian Government; of two others designated by the United States Consulate General; and of one president selected from among the consular body; no appeal to be allowed from their decision, and the tribunal to be appointed within one week from this date—the three months to be reckoned from the day of its appointment.

ALEXANDRIA, *August 8th*, 1864.

No. 56.

Mr. Dainese to Mr. Seward.

[No. 57.] ALEXANDRIA, *27th August*, 1864.

SIR: By my despatch of the 12th instant, No. 56, I apprized the Department of the interference which prevented the conclusion of the favorable arrangement proposed by the Egyptian government through Mr. Tastu, agent and consul general of France.

I have since been informed by Mr. Cumins that His Highness the Viceroy's railroad director sent for, settled, and paid him on the 31st ult. his claim—one in the list presented against the Egyptian government.

This, whilst of itself an acknowledgment of the wrong done Mr. Cumins, is also a proof that my demonstration had the good effect of prompting a beginning of redress. The other claims in that list would likewise have been settled had not said interference and the subsequent events hereinafter stated ruined my plans.

Mr. Hale arrived here the night of 17th to 18th instant. He handed me no instructions from the department, but only showed his commission. *I gave him hospitality*, made him acquainted with the particulars of the difficulty, and showed him that the only thing now required for securing the advantageous conditions I had been offered through Mr. Tastu, was for him to continue, through that gentleman, the negotiations commenced with me. He expressed his doubts as to whether a consul could haul down his flag; to which I observed that rule seven forbade it not to *diplomatic agents*, which was the official character of the incumbent of his office, and that as I did it to sustain the national honor upon a refusal of reparation for violation of domicil and insult to the Consulate, I did not suppose government would disapprove of it, *especially as a like course is pursued in Egypt in similar cases by all foreign agents,* and *was sanctioned by Mr. Webster*, while Secretary of State, in 1852, when Mr. McCauley hauled down his flag for a similar case. I called his attention to last winter's correspondence between this agency and the foreign office; to the protest of 9th February against the Egyptian government, illustrative of Mr. Thayer's quasi rupture with it for its repeated injustice to American interests, and added that at any rate no blame could attach to him in case of disapproval of said act, it being the work of others; and *as it had already* produced the good moral effect desired for our standing in Egypt, and induced advantageous offers for the immediate settlement of all pending claims, there was no good public reason for him to destroy, by changing his *programme* at this time, the prestige already produced, and thereby abandon these advantages. Our missionaries and protégés spoke in the same sense, insisting upon his sustaining my course, and he promised to do so.

On the following day, the 19th, Mr. Hale asked me to notify his appointment to the consular body, and inform them that he would on that day assume the duties of the consulate. I reminded him of rule 316, advising this *only* after the recognition by the local government of the new incumbent; and observed that if done beforehand it might offend the Viceroy and embarrass his colleagues; but he insisted, and I had to sign the usual circulars *which he dictated, putting the title "honorable" before his name.* He then took charge of and sent them round.

On the same day, upon producing authority therefor, Mr. Hale received from me, according to inventory transmitted to Mr. Thayer, and by him to the department in despatch No. 49, the cash balance, less expenses and fees, and the chattels of Mr. March's estate, taken care of and settled by me as acting vice consul for Cairo, under Mr. Thayer's instructions.

On the next and subsequent days, Mr. Hale had eight or ten secret interviews in my parlor with a Jew banker, named Landeau, which, it would seem, influenced and brought about the adoption of a course different from that agreed on, as instead of seeing Mr. Tastu and continuing the negotiations through him, he entered in communication, through Landeau, with Cherif Pacha, called on, and received the latter in my parlor on the 22d instant, and on the 23d ditto raised the U. S. flag, *without reparation or the settlement of pending claims.* It is alleged that he even promised not to sustain any, or at least, the most important ones amongst these.

Mr. Hale's course, as above, is looked upon and publicly denounced as having been dictated by motives of private interest, for the very comprehensive reason that it involves the unnecessary sacrifice of national honor and the ruin of the interests of our protégés, who, for their attachment to the Union, quite recently exhibited by their liberal donation through me to its defenders, deserve better treatment. It has even revived the old clamor against him for an intrigue attributed to him in former times, while he acted as a clerk or assistant to Mr. Thayer, in 1862, and Mr. Vice Consul Wilkinson, whereby it is affirmed that they obtained from the late Viceroy, Said Pacha, a present of fifty thousand dollars, or ten thousand pounds sterling, on a promise not to prosecute Sorian's and Kindineco's claims.

As a citizen and a christian, I deem it a duty to bring these facts to the knowledge of the Government, and to submit that public opinion, manifested both verbally and by means of prints and caricatures, may be respected, Mr. Hale's conduct investigated, and the wrongs arising therefrom remedied.

To make you to judge of the feeling here, I enclose one of these caricatures; it represents the United States flag as being pulled up *by the weight of gold!!!*

I must also apprise the Department that Mr. Hale, though my guest, regardless of my ill health, and in defiance of honor, right, or law, took possession of everything in my private house, both official and private, including Mr. Thayer's chattels, leaving untouched *only my two private retiring rooms*, which, being locked, he could not enter.

In extending hospitality to him, I assigned one bed-room

for his exclusive use, and permitted him to receive his guests in my parlor. I did not suppose a United States Consul could thus play the part of an "usurper" officially.

I am, sir, respectfully, your obedient servant,

(Signed) F. DAINESE.

Hon. W. H. SEWARD,
Secretary of State.

No. 57.

Mr. Dainese to Mr Seward.

[No. 58.] ALEXANDRIA, *September* 17, 1864.

SIR: In my despatch of the 27th ult., No. 57, I informed the Department of such matters of a public nature as I deemed it my duty to present for its consideration, and of Mr. Hale's encroachments in my own private house, where he had been hospitably entertained as a guest. Following these encroachments, he, on the 13th instant, broke into my private apartments and plundered their contents. In them were furniture, money, and important papers, of all of which he robbed me. Had there been a court of justice here, I should have arraigned him before it; but as, on the strength of his Consular commission, he plays the despot in Egypt, I can neither hinder his depredations nor obtain redress for them; and I am, therefore, compelled to appeal, as I now do, to my Government. I possess, in support of the charge I have brought against Mr. Hale, the affidavit of an eye witness, which I will produce in due time, and at the proper moment. I also hold a second affidavit, with reference to the promise of another eye witness, "to testify to the perpetration of this unwarrantable violence, if called upon to do so before a court," but who hesitates, while in Egypt, to sign any paper likely to be seen by Mr. Hale, for fear it might injure his interests. I could, with ease, obtain proofs against Mr. Hale from many other quarters concerning this and other delinquencies, were the witnesses not in fear of persecution, as he boasts of the unlimited powers he possesses, and asserts that all he does is by order of Government. His powers are in fact *great* here "*for sacrificing American* interests and ill treating Americans," as he is readily assisted in doing so by the local government since he placed himself in its power.

Mr. Hale also took possession, without previous notice, of the Vice-Consular office at Cairo, hitherto in my charge, in consequence of Mr. Taylor's non-arrival, and wrongfully retains the furniture and other things in it, paid for by me to Mr. Wilkinson and others; and he further declines reimbursing the sums paid by me for freight and charges on nine boxes of his private chattels sent to my care and delivered to him on his arrival, and for the postage on his private letters and telegrams, on the ridiculous pretext that I must claim the amount from Government.

Expecting due redress for all these grievances, I am, sir, respectfully, your obedient servant,

(Signed) F. DAINESE.

Hon. W. H. Seward,
Secretary of State.

No. 58.

Mr. Dainese to Mr. Seward.

[No. 59.] Alexandria, *September 24th*, 1864.

Sir: In confirmation of my dispatch of the 17th inst., No. 58, I beg leave to inform the Department, that Mr. Hale's clerk has just handed me a letter from Hon. S. P. Chase, which Mr. Hale had previously *opened*, and then placed in another envelope addressed to me in his own hand writing. Another letter from Mr. Purser H. Pangborn, which states to be enclosed in one from Captain Stellwagen, was likewise sent to me, opened by Mr. Hale, who scrupled not to keep that from the captain, and assigned no reason for so unheard of a proceeding. Other letters sent by and to me are astray, and Mr. Hale's action in the two above-mentioned instances, would seem to explain their absence.

The interception of my correspondence by Mr. Hale, may have serious consequences and I hereby file my solemn protest against the official who, by force of his position, has been enabled to commit such an action.

In addition to this, Mr. Hale compels people into his presence, and employs every means to obtain *ex parte* statements to my detriment. He also endeavors, in every manner possible, to annoy me and injure my reputation by false statements, and he accounts for the undisguised malice of his behaviour, by alleging it to be, falsely as I suppose, in pursuance of instructions from the Department.

The object of our consular establishment is the protection of Americans and of their interests abroad, and as Mr. Hale is fast ruining them—as there is sufficient evidence to show—I can see no reason for burdening the Treasury with the expense of retaining him here; any representative of a friendly foreign power would, as a matter of international courtesy, protect American interests far better than he does.

The outcry against him is general, and many of our "protégés" have already abandoned American protection as worthless.

His confidential man and go-between, (a Greek whom Mr. Thayer would not even admit into his presence,) went round to collect signatures in his master's favor, but unluckily for the success of the scheme, not one of the reputable men in Alexandria would allow his name to be used for such a purpose; such facts are anything but creditable to our great country, and the Department will have but little difficulty, by the means at its disposal, in verifying the exactitude of my statement.

I am, sir, respectfully, your obedient servant,

(Signed) F. DAINESE.

HON. W. H. SEWARD,
Secretary of State.

No. 59.

Mr. Dainese to President Lincoln.

To his Excellency the President of the United States:

MR. PRESIDENT: In continuation of my memorial of the

18th of last December, I have the honor to state that since my return to this country I have learnt that, subsequently to my departure from Alexandria, Mr. Hale, although well aware that I was coming home, and that my domicil is Washington, with a view to injure me, took the liberty of attaching certain machinery, &c., which had been left by me with a friend in Egypt for sale, his pretext for this step being that I was indebted to certain parties in the United States, and was either unwilling or unable to pay just claims.

Now, I deny owing any one a single cent, the payment of which I would refuse, and challenge any one alleging to have claims upon me to produce them, either to me or before the courts at Washington; and whilst I most solemnly protest against Mr. Hale's conduct, I also respectfully request that he be directed to remove instantly any attachments which he may have made arbitrarily on property left by me in Egypt, and that he abstain hereafter from meddling in any way with my affairs, or interfering in any way with me. Proud and glad as I always have been and shall be of the protection of the American flag, I had rather not see its influence turned to my detriment under the auspices of such mal-administrators as Mr. Hale.

Nor am I the only sufferer from his misdeeds. In support of the assertion contained in despatch No. 57 to the State Department, copy of which I enclosed in my memorial of the 18th of December, to the effect "that Mr. Hale had sacrificed and would continue to sacrifice American interests," I can now show that he has deliberately done so by withdrawing protection from and delivering over to the tender mercies of the Egyptian rulers Messrs. Kindineco and Santi; the former a respectable merchant, and the latter the editor of the only American journal in Egypt, who displeased Mr. Hale by his free expositions of liberal ideas, and by denouncing his conduct with reference to the flag.*

* When Mr. Hale delivered his address to the Viceroy, and withdrew American protection from Kindineco and Santi, his minister for foreign affairs wrote

This I submit to have been a violation of law and of the policy enunciated by our Government in Mr. Marcy's letter

---

the following circular to the consuls general of foreign powers, residing in Egypt, viz:

(Translated Copy.)

"CAIRO, *5th November*, 1864.

"MR. CONSUL GENERAL: American nationality having, by order of the President of the United States, been withdrawn from Messrs. Kindineco and Joseph Santi, it is my duty to inform you that the Egyptian Government will not recognize, in future, as belonging to any other nationality, or as depending, in any cause, from any other protection, Mr. Kindineco, who was once a local subject, then an Austrian, and lastly an American, and Mr. Santi, who lately relinquished his Italian nationality to become an American citizen.

"Without reminding you of occurrences still too recent to be forgotten, I am convinced, Mr. Consul General, that you will not hesitate to coöperate in the moral(*a*) measure just taken by the Egyptian Government, which I now notify to you.

"I will thank you to inform your government of this, adding such explanations as you may think proper, and which are of public notoriety.

"Accept, Mr. Consul General, the assurances of my high consideration.

("Signed) CHERIF PACHA,

The Minister for Foreign Affairs."

---

a The moral measure above alluded to, was *buying off* these two men's lives and property. Mr. Kindineco received a printed copy of the above circular, and transmitted it to President Lincoln with his following

Petition, which his death left unacted upon:

"Mr. PRESIDENT: I have received from Alexandria the enclosed copy of a circular from the Egyptian Minister for Foreign Affairs to foreign consuls in Egypt, wherein is stated that, by your order, American nationality is withdrawn from me.

"This was secretly arranged with Mr. Charles Hale, our Consul General, for a large bribe, and was carried out without previous notice to me.

"I am, at the same time, informed that, simultaneously to the issue of that circular, the Egyptian Government took possession of my property, demolished one hundred and seventy shops belonging to me, and it otherwise persecutes my family and my interests in Egypt.

"Your high reputation for justice assures me that a similar order did not emanate from you, as I have given no cause to be thus sold off to my persecutors by the very country of my adoption; and I hereby bring the fact to your knowledge, begging for the adoption of such immediate measures as may save from the vindictiveness and barbarity of the Egyptian rulers the lives of my family, unconscienciously sold to them by Mr. Hale, and restore my property and rights.

"I am, Mr. President, with the highest respect, your most humble servant,

("Signed) THOS. N. KINDINECO."

Later Mr. Kindineco filed with President Johnson the following affidavit:

No. 60.

STATE OF NEW YORK, }
City and County of New York, } *ss.*

Thomas N. Kindineco being duly sworn says, that in the year 1864, and for several years previous, he had been doing business in Egypt, under the protection of the American government, having in the year 1861 taken steps to become a citizen of the United States, by declaring his intention according to law.

on the Costa affair, published, with comments thereon, in Wheaton's 6th Edition, page 128, and sequel. Its immedi-

---

And this affiant further says, that he had a large claim against the Egyptian government for moneys formerly due him, and also violation of his domicil, and the destruction of his property and business, and for personal insults to himself, all of which was in a fair way of adjustment under the administration of Francis Dainese, Esq., then acting Consul General of the United States in Egypt.

This affiant further says, that in the spring of 1862, Charles Hale, at present Consul General of the United States in Egypt, but who at that time acted under Mr. Consul Thayer, for a large bribe, as this affiant verily believes, impeded and prevented the prosecution of his former claim; and that upon his arrival at Alexandria, in 1864, as Consul General, without cause and in violation of the rights of this affiant and of the plainest principles of justice, and as this affiant believes, in consideration of an additional large bribe paid to him by the Viceroy of Egypt, he, the said Hale, dismissed this affiant's claims, and wrongfully withdrew the protection of the United States government from this affiant, leaving him and his family to the mercy of his enemies and of the hirelings of the Egyptian government.

That said Hale falsely pretended and gave out that he had done this under the orders and directions of the President of the United States, and thereby abandoned this affiant and his family and property to the mercy of the local rulers, who immediately took possession of his real estate, demolished several of his buildings, from which he was receiving annual rents of two thousand pounds sterling, and otherwise perpetrated all kinds of wrongs upon his family, and ruining him completely in his pecuniary affairs. This affiant further says, that all this was done and suffered to be done by said Hale, as this affiant believes, in consideration of bribes received by him from the Viceroy of Egypt, and that he is now, in consequence of said acts, a refugee from said country, deprived of his family and his property by reason of the wicked and scandalous conduct of said Hale.

(Signed) THOMAS N. KINDINECO.

Sworn and subscribed to, before me, this 12th day of August, 1865.

(Signed) EDWIN F. CORREY, Jr.,
Notary Public for the State of New York.

[Stamp.] (Official seal of Edwin F. Correy, Jr.)

District of Columbia, }
Washington County, } *to wit.*

I do hereby certify, that I have compared the forgoing affidavit and statement with the original, and find it to be a true copy.

Witness my hand and seal, this 16th day of August, A. D. 1865.

JOHN H. GODDARD, *J. P.* [Seal.]

Subsequently Mr. Kindineco served upon Mr. Seward and the other parties the following protest, viz:

No. 61.

United States of America, }
State of New York, } *ss.*
City and County of New York, }

Be it remembered that on this 10th day of October, A. D. 1865, before me, Charles Nettleton, a notary public in and for the State of New York, duly commissioned and sworn, and dwelling in said city of New York, personally appeared Thomas Kindineco, now of the said city of New York, who, being by me duly sworn, doth depose and say as follows:

That he, in the year of our Lord 1865, in due form of law, declared his inate consequence was the forcible stoppage by the Egyptian Government of Santi's paper, his own imprisonment, and

---

tention of becoming a citizen of the United States and of having his domicil therein, became entitled to and since then enjoyed the protection of the government of the United States.

The deponent had business engagements as a merchant in Egypt, and has a large claim against the Egyptian Government for losses sustained by him on account of the seizure, by the said government of Egypt, of certain property, the nonfulfilment of a grant for the supply of lumber to the said government of Egypt for the space of five years, (a large portion of which lumber was cut, and is now rotting on the Macedonian hills,) for the subsequent violation of his premises in Egypt, on the 15th day of July, A. D. 1864, and for destruction of his property, and other acts of injustice against him by said government, proof whereof is in his possession, and also on file at the office of the United States Consul General in Egypt, and for the settlement of which said claims an arrangement had been agreed upon, and was about to be carried out in the early part of August, 1864, between the Viceroy of Egypt and Mr. Dainese, the United States acting consul general there;

That before the said arrangement and settlement of deponent's said claims was consummated, one Charles Hale, appointed by the United States Government to be consul general for Egypt, arrived in Alexandria, in the place and stead of the acting consul general who arranged the settlement thereof;

That said Charles Hale repudiated the act of his predecessor in office, so far as deponent was concerned, and not only refused to take action in the matter on behalf of deponent, but dismissed his deponent's claim, and illegally concocted the taking of and surrendered an additional landed property at Fort Napoleon to the Viceroy, and illegally, cruelly, and wrongfully withdrew from deponent the protection of the United States, which he, until then, had enjoyed, using—and, as the deponent is informed—*falsely* using the name of the President of the United States as the authority for such the acts of him said Hale; and deponent says that he verily believes that said Hale was actuated in doing so by private considerations and pecuniary personal interest, and that so it will appear on an investigation being had.

And deponent further says, that by reason of such connivances of the United States consul (said Charles Hale) with the Viceroy of Egypt, and of the information conveyed to him, that attempts were being made against his life—thus left exposed to the mercy of the Viceroy—and failing in his efforts to move Consul Hale to more humane acts, he was compelled to quit Egypt and proceed to the United States for redress, leaving behind him considerable property, both real and personal, including a large amount of valuable machinery and agricultural implements of American manufacture, which had been consigned to him by the manufacturers. And deponent says that after his departure, the Egyptian Government seized additional property belonging to him, and demolished several tenements from which he received large rents, and that he has, for the above reasons, large claims against the Egyptian Government, which are now outstanding and unliquidated, whereof deponent requires me to protest, requiring an act thereof from me when and where needful and necessary: whereupon I, the said notary public, at the request aforesaid, do, by these presents, join with the said deponent, and both of us do hereby solemnly swear, protest against the cruel oppression and wrong he has suffered at the hands of the Egyptian Government; and also solemnly protest against the unlawful, cruel, and malicious abandonment of deponent by the said Charles Hale, as the United States consul general at Alexandria aforesaid, and claim to hold said Egyptian Government and said Charles Hale, jointly and severally, liable to make good to deponent all loss and damage which has already accrued, or which may hereafter accrue, to him by reason or means of the acts of the Egyptian Government and the said Charles Hale respectively, as herein appears.

the gutting and destruction of his office, and demolition by the police of shops and other buildings belonging to Mr. Kindineco.

And deponent alleges that while the protection of the United States Government was extended to him he was successfully introducing goods of American manufacture to the Egyptian markets, and that the consumption of such goods was steadily increasing; but that when he was compelled, as herein appears, to leave the said country of Egypt, the development of commercial intercourse between this country and Egypt was obstructed and impeded to the public loss and detriment.

And deponent submits that he is entitled to the interference in his behalf of the Government of the United States, to enable him to enforce the said claims against the Government of Egypt and whomsoever it may concern, and to obtain payment thereof, and respectfully entreats that all necessary and proper steps may be taken by the United States Government, and directions given with that end and intent, and that reference may be had to the said proofs and evidence in the possession and also on file in the office of the consulate general in Alexandria aforesaid.

And deponent submits this protest for the consideration of the United States Government, and hereby requires official copies thereof to be notified to the Viceroy of Egypt and to Consul General Hale, at Alexandria, in order that they may severally take notice of the same; and deponent hereby declares that he will at all times and places, whenever and wherever the offenders may be brought to account for the wrongful acts as hereintofore deposed to, use the same against them and each of them, and all others concerned, and that a like copy be delivered to him, and one communicated to the State Department at Washington, for the ends of right and justice. And in testimony of the truth of the premises, the said deponent has hereunto set his hand.

THOMAS KINDINECO.

Thus done and protested by me, the said notary public, at the city of New York, county and State of New York, this 10th day of October, A. D. 1865.

[SEAL.] CHAS. NETTLETON,
Notary Public in and for the city, county, and State of New York,
[STAMP.] *No.* 111 *Broadway.*

And I certify that in pursuance of the foregoing request, three copies of the above protest were made, and that each copy had appended thereto the following certificates, and were dealt with as by the certificate in that behalf appears.

STATE OF NEW YORK,
City and County of New York, } *ss:*

I, Charles Nettleton, a Notary Public in and for the city, county, and State of New York, do hereby certify that I have this day examined and compared the foregoing copy of an instrument of protest, of which it purports to be a copy, and that the same is a true and correct copy of the said original instrument of protest, and of each and every part thereof. And I further certify that the said original instrument of protest is duly registered in my office at No. 111 Broadway, in the city of New York; and this copy is hereby notified to the foregoing named Viceroy of Egypt, (or Charles Hale, or the Secretary of State for the United States of America, as the case may be.)

In witness whereof, I have hereunto set my hand and affixed my notarial seal, this 11th day of October, A. D. 1865.

(Signed) CHARLES NETTLETON,
Notary Public, in and for the City, County and State of New York.

Something, too, might well be said of the rank discourtesy shown by Mr. Hale on his arrival to that eminent

---

STATE OF NEW YORK,
City and County of New York, } *ss:*

I hereby certify that a copy of the foregoing protest, duly certified as above, was served upon the Secretary of the United States of America, the Viceroy of Egypt, and Charles Hale, the United States Consul General for Egypt at Alexandria, and each of them. As to the service upon the Secretary of State of the United States, by addressing such copy upon him, to him, on the outside thereof, and enclosing the same in an envelope, securely sealed, and such envelope having addressed on the outside "To the Honorable William H. Seward, Secretary of State, Washington, D. C.," and endorsed "Official Business," and signed by me on the outside, and depositing such envelope in the post office in the city of New York, on the 12th day of October, A. D. 1865, postage paid. As to the service upon the Viceroy of Egypt, by addressing such copy served upon him, to him, on the outside thereof, and enclosing the same in an envelope securely sealed up, and such envelope being addressed on the outside thereof "To the Viceroy of Egypt, at Alexandria, Egypt," and endorsed "Official Business," and signed by me on the outside thereof, and, on the 12th day of October, A. D. 1865, depositing such envelope in the post office at the city of New York, postage paid. And as to the service upon the said Charles Hale, the United States Consul at Egypt, at Alexandria, by addressing such copy, so served upon him, to him, on the outside thereof, and enclosing the same in an envelope securely fastened, and such envelope being addressed on the outside thereof "To Charles Hale, Esq., United States Consul General for Egypt, at Alexandria, Egypt," and endorsed "Official Business," and signed by me on the outside thereof, and, on the 12th day of October, A. D. 1865, depositing such envelope in the post office, in the city of New York, and, at the same time, paying the postage thereon. And I further certify that I have this day handed to the foregoing named Thomas Kindineco the original of the above-mentioned protest.

In testimony whereof, I have hereunto set my hand and affixed my notarial seal, this 12th day of October, A. D. 1865.

[Five-cent stamp.] CHARLES NETTLETON, *Notary Public*,
[SEAL.] 111 *Broadway, New York City.*

No. 62.

To the Honorables Ira Harris and E. D. Morgan, Senators, and to our Representatives from the State of New York:

GENTLEMEN: The undersigned Merchants and Manufacturers, representing several millions of dollars capital, and controlling a large amount of labor, beg respectively to call your attention to the petition of Thomas Kindineco, setting forth certain grievances and impediments to his commerce in Egypt.

Having been in business connection with him, we can testify as to the honorability of his transactions, and assure you that we are all losers in our export trade of agricultural implements and machinery for Egypt by the acts he complains of.

We, therefore, gentlemen, in the interest of American inventions and commerce, and, above all, for the honor, integrity, justice, and fair fame, which we should uphold before the eyes of the world, and the protection which a great and powerful Republic owes to its citizens introducing its productions abroad, pray that you, as our representatives, have the case of Mr. Kindineco so thor-

French consular officer, Mr. Tastu, whose friendly and successful efforts at conciliation I brought to the notice of the Department, but which were ignored by Mr. Hale in the most unheard of manner.

---

oughly investigated that there may be neither delay nor excuse for refusing him justice and proper protection for the pursuit of American trade in Egypt.

With sentiments of consideration, we have the honor, gentlemen, to be your constituents and obedient servants.

WM. D. ANDREWS & BRO.,
Pump and Engine Manufacturers, 414 *Water Street, New York.*
BAYLEY & HILL,
Rotary Pump and Fire Engine Manufacturers, 58 *John Street, New York.*
FRANKLIN H. LUMMUS & CO.,
New York Cotton Gin Company, 82 *John Street, New York.*
CHAS. A. BUCKLEY, *Treasurer,*
Atlas Manufacturing Company, Cotton Gin, &c., 26 *and* 28 *Barclay St., N. Y.*
E. H. REEVES & CO.,
Agricultural Implements, 187 *Water Street, New York.*
HORACE L. EMERY & SON,
Albany Agricultural Works, Albany. New York,
Sample Room and Depot, 184 *Water Street, New York,*
Manufacturers of H. Powers' Cotton Gins, Presses, &c., &c.
WHEELER, MELICK & CO.,
Agricultural Implements, Cor. Hamilton and Liberty Streets, Albany.

No. 63.

This nineteenth day of November, in the year of our Lord eighteen hundred and sixty-three, in the presence of Messrs. E. A. Diamandidi and T. N. Kindineco, having requested Mr. Robert Wilkinson, heretofore United States Vice-consul for Cairo, to surrender the consular archives removed by him from the consular office to some unknown place, said Wilkinson refused to do so, alleging, as his reason, that he had the right to hold the consulate, having paid for it. Moreover, that, when in the early part of the year eighteen hundred and sixty-two he received from the late Viceroy, Said Pacha, the present of ten thousand pounds sterling, and paid two-thirds thereof to Mr. Charles Hale, then acting in behalf of the Consulate General, it was on the express understanding and solemn promise "that he, Wilkinson, should hold the office of Vice Consul for Cairo until the expiration of Mr. Thayer's consular term," that he handed over the money to said Charles Hale. That if this promise be now violated all these moneys should be repaid to him, and that he would retain the archives until this question was settled. He, the said Wilkinson, added further that he had apprised Mr. Colquhoun, British Consul General, of these facts, and is ready to bring the matter to a trial before the British court, from which he depends.

Cairo, this nineteenth day of November, in the year of our Lord one thousand eight hundred and sixty-three.

(Signed) E. A. DIAMANDIDI, T. N. KINDINECO, } Attest.

Attested to before me,
(Signed) F. DAINESE,
[L. S.] *Acting U. S. Consul General for Egypt.*

In confirmation of the assertions alluded to in the despatch before mentioned, to the effect that as far back as the

---

No. 64.

Mr. Hale's Letter to Mr. Thayer.

(I write this in Abbott's room in the Department of State, immediately after my interview with the Secretary.)

WASHINGTON, D. C., 1st *November*, 1862.

DEAR THAYER: I wrote to you from Boston on the 28th of October. The same afternoon I started for Washington. Upon the train at Worcester I was joined by Theodore C. Ketchen, of Littleton, who for a while, you remember, belonged to the class of 1850. He gave me an amusing account of affairs at Littleton. Thattuch Hartwell has become very unpopular by his greed for office, (having successfully sought the office of postmaster, with fifty dollars per annum;) and our *Wood*, after being acquitted on a trial under the bastardy act, brought by a young woman who had served in his house, scandalized the community by marrying another Irish servant woman of his household.

On the train from New York to Philadelphia and Washington, I found Frank Fiske, looking pretty well, although evidently not strong. He was much interested in hearing about you. He was not in uniform, and was not coming to join his regiment, but to transact some business at the Department—I believe, to resign; at least he told me such was his intention. I advised against it; I don't know whether he carried it out; I called to see him, last night, but found he had gone home.

I arrived in Washington Wednesday evening (29.) On repairing to the Department of State the next day, I found it closed, pursuant to a new rule, whereby it is always closed on Thursdays to all but foreign ministers and their secretaries. I went into the Treasury, however, and called upon Underwood, the Fifth Auditor. He remembered me at once, having seen me in the Speaker's chair in Boston. He expressed great interest in you, and said you were an admirable consul. After conversation, I said you had requested me to inquire if there were anything in your accounts requiring explanation, and, if so, I could probably clear it up. He said there was nothing to be explained. I pressed the point, and said perhaps I had best see the clerk having them in charge, as possibly there might be something requiring remark. He said, not at all; he (Underwood) had looked at them himself, and found everything regular and proper. "We have allowed everything in the accounts," said he. "Although in one quarter the miscellaneous account was somewhat large, I consulted the Secretary of State and received directions to allow the whole. It is all right," he repeated, "and Mr. Thayer need give himself no uneasiness about his accounts." Underwood desired to be remembered kindly to you when I should write.

The next day I went to the State Department, and, after seeing Abbott, saw Chilton, who was pleased to hear of you, and repeated his encomium on the value of your services. Through him I asked an interview with Mr. Seward. Mr. Seward had gone to a cabinet meeting, but Fred. Seward said his father would be happy to see me at any time, either at his house or at the Department.

I called upon Mr. Forrest, the clerk having charge of the passport office, and could find no record of any passport having been granted to Kindineco, either at Washington or New York. I carefully looked through the whole list myself, (which was voluminous,) from July, 1861, to February, 1862, and could not find the name. By sending the date and number of the passport they can at once tell here if it is genuine.

In the evening I called at Mr. Seward's house. The servant said that he was very particularly engaged; that he regretted this, and wished to be excused, and would be pleased to have me call at the Department the next morning.

early part of 1862, he had sacrificed for hire the interest of Mr. Kindineco and other "protégés," whilst acting as Mr.

Accordingly, this morning I came again to the Department, and after the usual waiting time, was admitted to Mr. Seward's presence. This interview, you understand, is with the Secretary of State himself. He received me very cordially, and complimented me on my improved appearance. He spoke most kindly of you, and said you made a most excellent Consul General. I brought up the subject of protégés, which he said he perfectly understood; that he had already written you what would be entirely satisfactory to you, and that you might be sure you would receive no instructions that would make you any trouble in such matters.

That times were changed. A few years ago, perhaps, we could afford to listen to requests to take up cases of persons having claims and grievances. *Now*, we have first to look at the paramount interests of our own country, laboring in a crisis; and in our foreign relations, we must study to give the least possible trouble to friendly powers. That this principle governed his correspondence, not only with you, but with all our representatives abroad. That he uniformly wrote that distressed Americans must come home, and not make trouble abroad. The present is not a proper time to redress their real or fancied grievances.

With regard to Kindineco, he said he remembered him perfectly; that he came to him bearing a letter of introduction from one of our foreign ministers, he believed the minister of Turin. I asked him if he had not confounded Lattis with Kindineco; he said, no; Kindineco was recommended, as he had said. He requested K. to make a brief of his case, which he did. On receiving it, he (Mr. Seward) found it too vague and general, and told him so. Kindineco said it would be difficult to make it more specific, and that was the last he (Mr. S.) had seen or heard of him.

I told Mr S. the character of K., and he said he should of course not recommend his case to you, except on conclusive grounds.

In conformity with your particular request, entered in my note-book, I then mentioned the subject of the title agent and consul general, telling Mr. Seward that that title had been assumed by all your predecessors, and was assumed by the other representatives of the great powers, and asking him if there would be any objections to your using it. He asked, "What is the title in the law?" and I told him I believed the law only spoke of a Consul General.

He said he supposed the law regulated the matter; at any rate he could not confer a title unknown to the law; that if you found it advisable to assume the title he should probably never hear of it, and if he did, probably should make no objection, but he had no right to authorize you to use it.

On repeating all this conversation immediately afterwards to Chilton, he said if he were in your place he would not hesitate to use the title.

Mr. Seward closed the interview by renewing the assurance that the views of the Department were such as would save you all trouble and annoyance in dealing with protégés and claimants, and by expressing his pleasure in finding me returned to America in such good health.

When he spoke above of the letter he had written, I suppose he alluded to the answer to the big despatch in Lattis's case—of course I did not tell him I had seen that.

A very large number of documents will be sent into Congress this year relating to foreign affairs. Among them will be included the Viceroy's letter to the President. Chilton had your despatch covering this lying upon the table.

Your despatch concerning the commerce, etc., will be included in the volume of commercial regulations, and care will be taken to correct the misprint of "Vice" for *ice* among the principal articles received into Egypt from America.

Chilton says that he has already forwarded to you the copies of documents needed to complete your archives, and that he took great pleasure in doing so.

Thayer's assistant, I beg to enclose copy of a letter of his to Mr. Thayer, from which it was evident that he was in-

I tried to call upon Dainese at the National, but found him gone out west. Fiske told me that Dainese's plan in going to Egypt was to get a commission to come back as representative of the Porte or of the Pacha near Washington. Abbott told me that he thought if you had any business with the Department instead of writing to Dainese you had best write direct to him (A.) or to Chilton, for that D. is not liked at the Department; all of which I tell you in confidence for what it is worth.

With regard to Salvago's wish to be appointed "Consul" at Syra (instead of Consular Agent,) I learn at this Department that it is the settled policy to refuse new appointments as consuls to any persons who are not citizens of the United States; that the effect of such an application as is proposed would simply be, after the creation of the office of consul to cause a citizen to be appointed to fill it, which would turn S. right out. Accordingly it is best policy to let the matter rest for the present; after the war, perhaps something can be done.

I learn, accidentally, and in confidence, that the Consulate at Athens will be vacant on the 31st of December next; if the salary were larger (it is only $1,000) I should be tempted to apply for it myself.

Don't fail to send either to me, to Abbott, or to Chilton the number and date of Kindineco's passport.

Having completed, as far as I was able, the principal objects of my visit hither, I return by this afternoon's train. I shall pause in New York.

You must understand that the highest regard is felt for you by everybody here.

Seward, Underwood, Chilton, Abbott, they feel sure that you are emphatically the right man in the right place; whatever you do will be accepted as right *prima facie*, and they are much more likely to have to make explanations to you than you to them.

Chilton and Abbott desire to be particularly remembered. I told C. that I believed you were getting up a box for him. Perhaps I will write to you further about that.

Remember me to Lansing, Wilkinson and Salvago.

Yours, faithfully,

(Signed,) CHARLES HALE.

Remarks on Mr. Hale's letter to Mr. Consul General Thayer, dated Washington, November 1st, 1862.

The foregoing letter, given at length, is apparently a very earnest and friendly one from Mr. Hale to his old chief; still there pervades in the whole composition an under current of selfish diplomacy, and of willingness to injure others, which we trust to be enabled to analyze, and by doing so to place Mr. Hale in "impuris naturalibus" before the gaze of those whose sentiments of true honor would cause them to revolt from anything bearing the least resemblance to treachery and time-serving.

After serving up a little local scandal in a pleasant way, he proceeds to business, and is chiefly occupied by the interests and well-being of his friend Mr. Thayer; he has interviews with Messrs. Underwood, Abbott, and Chilton, and finally with Mr. Seward in person; but previously to this last visit he calls on Mr. Forrest, of the passport office, and can discover no passport registered in Mr. Kindineco's name, (who did then give the passport which is "en règle"?) and to do him justice, he appears throughout to have taken an extraordinary interest in Mr. Kindineco, although not always with a view to his advantage. We next find him listening to Mr. Seward's expositions of the foreign policy of America, (of the correctness of the statement concerning which Mr. Sew-

triguing and misinforming Mr. Seward with reference to Kindineco and others, in order to prevent any active intervention on the part of the Government in their behalf.

When, at a late date, Mr. Thayer became fully aware of the extensive injustice which had accrued to our "protégés" through the intrigues of his subordinate, he charged me, both verbally and in many letters, to prosecute their claims, and, in consequence of the personally offensive allusion to me contained in the letter in question, made it over to me to be used as I might think fit. Amongst Mr. Thayer's papers there were very many other letters from Mr. Hale and others, of a far more compromising character than the above, and the present production of which would be an unanswerable proof of guilt; but although I am aware of their contents, seeing that Mr. Thayer showed them to me in his life-

---

ard is of course the best judge,) and doing Mr. Kindineco the least possible good in the world by furnishing the Secretary of State with "an account of K's character," which evidently disinclined Mr. Seward to assist him.. Now, the gentleman whose name had escaped Mr. Seward's memory, and who had in the first instance recommended Mr. Kindineco to his protection, was Louis Kossuth, from whom Mr. K., at this moment, holds another letter of the same tenor, dated via Accademia, Turin, Italy, September 28th, 1864, and few who have the honor of personally knowing that noble-minded patriot will ever suppose him capable of committing himself to the extent of recommending an unknown or an unworthy person to the Premier of America.

The next person victimized by Mr. Hale is Mr. Dainese, to whom he attributes all sorts of intentions, and to whom he wishes Mr. Thayer not to write "because D was not liked at the Department."

That Mr. Thayer knew his man and fully appreciated his disinterested advice, was shown by the fact of his subsequently nominating this unsatisfactory person, Mr. D., to be his own trusted representative at Alexandria.

Putting this and that together—the letter before us and Mr. Hale's last epistle denying to Mr. Kindineco American nationality so soon as his position enabled him to do so—we ask whether he has acted throughout from purely patriotic motives, or whether the point-blank assertions of many of the folks at Alexandria are correct with reference to bribery?

Mr. Thayer was a trusted and tried officer of the Government whom Mr. Hale flattered during his lifetime, and if he thought fit to protect Kindineco, and to give over charge of his office to Mr. Dainese, we think Mr. Hale must have had strong reasons for acting in a contrary sense.

The charge of bribery in the spring of 1862 seems supported by affidavits corroborated by the following facts, namely:

That shortly after the time Mr. Hale is reported to have got the money from the Viceroy, he proceeded to Boston, bought the "Advertiser," and invested a large amount in stocks through Mr. Kidder, Messrs. John A. Thayer & Brothers' managing man; then under date 28th October, 1862, he wrote a letter to Mr. Thayer to the effect that he had invested in all $14,887 75 "from the moneys which I (he) brought out of Egypt."

time, I felt myself bound as a man of honor not to touch them after his decease, and to confine myself to the one he had given me; they were, with other effects, in my house when Mr. Hale forcibly took possession of it. (See despatch No. 57.)

Trusting in your well known sense of justice for redress, I have the honor to be, Mr. President, your most obedient servant,

(Signed) F. DAINESE.

WASHINGTON, *February* 25, 1865.

No. 65.

Mr. Dainese to President Johnson.

To the President of the United States:

MR. PRESIDENT: I have the honor to submit the following statement of facts, which transpired last fall at Alexandria, in Egypt, and which involve grave misconduct on the part of Mr. Charles Hale, then and now Consul General of the United States to Egypt. In this statement I shall confine myself to facts which are either within my own knowledge, or are set forth in affidavits, dispatches, and official documents, already on file in the Executive Mansion, and of which copies are hereto appended:

[A full report is here given of the facts stated in my letters to President Lincoln, of 18th December, 1864, and 25th February, 1865, accompanied by copies of said letters, and their enclosures, all which precede in this appendix, and the reproduction of which is here omitted to avoid repetition.]

I learned further that Mr. Hale reinstated, after my departure, three consular agents dismissed by me for dealing in slaves, and for whose dismissal I was highly complimented by the Viceroy's Government. (See letter L to the President, &c.)

I informed the President, by letters of 25th and 28th February, 1865, of these additional facts, accompanied by the proper documents in support thereof. (See papers L and M.) In the crowd of business at that time I could not secure his attention until his return from Richmond, when his assassination prevented his acting on the subject. These facts will account for the delay in presenting to your notice events which transpired over half a year ago. As a citizen of the United States, I have felt it my duty to expose acts so disgraceful to our nation, and use my privilege to appeal to you for the vindication of my rights when they are so grossly violated; and while I will not presume to suggest the duty of the government to recall or punish an unfaithful representative, and vindicate the national honor and the rights of those for whose protection the faith of the government is pledged, I claim the right respectfully to ask that my rights of person and property as a citizen be protected; that the hand which has stayed my business be removed; that my property be restored, in its original value, and the injuries I have suffered be redressed by the arm of the Executive, which is the only power strong enough to promptly reach the offender.

I have the honor to be, with high respect, your obedient servant,

F. DAINESE.

WASHINGTON, *June* 12, 1865.

No. 66.

Translation of extract from the Italo-Egyptian Journal "Il Popalo." Edited by Mr. Santi.

The independent banner of the U. S. of America, which spreads abroad its stars as symbols of splendor and beauty, now waves draped with crape and bound with a chain of iron, a standing proof of the ignominy inflicted on America by its new representative! C. Hale, who passed the seas as the supposed champion of liberty, but who is, nevertheless, the upholder of despotism, has sold himself as an agent to carry out the despotic will of others. At the very moment when the honor of the American flag should have been preserved, and when Mr. Dainese was vindicating the honor of America, offended by the local government, the narrow mind of C. Hale intermeddles and indecently disturbs the question, encroaches on the rights of third parties, and casts a slur on the free and noble nation of which he is the accredited representative, reducing his country in public opinion, to the position of a weak and degraded power, *the least amongst the least!*

Oh! could the shadow of Washington arise once more! indignation would possess him, and with an angry hand he would send back this partisan of slavery to the dark dens of those whose trade it is to conspire against freedom!

A careful consideration of this scandalous affair will lead us to no explanations of it but those to be found in great self-interested views or in a culpable disposition to act wrongfully; tendencies, which, impossible as they may seem, are but too prevalent amongst creatures who seem destined to be rejected by the whole human race.

There are, however, winds that scatter the strongest men and their machinations like a handful of dust; and we therefore believe that, ere long, there will issue from America, that land of liberty and unsullied popular rights, those words of reprehension with which she never fails to crush and humiliate such of her degenerate sons, shameless helots as they are, who traverse the world in her name and make common cause with those who insult the sacred cause for the maintenace of which so much blood has been shed.

We hope, then, soon to see a speedy termination to all such abominations, and that Mr. Hale, dismissed from his public charge, may be sent to seek, within the walls of some temple, an inspiration to better actions from the sacred principles of the Bible.

He would, at least, be more in place there than here.

No. 67.

To the PRESIDENT:

Subsequent to the insult offered last summer to the United States consulate general in Egypt by the local police, and for which satisfaction was demanded and about to be obtained by me, then acting consul general, a similar insult was offered to certain Italian residents at that place.

The demand for redress of insult to America was corruptly abandoned by Mr. Hale on his arrival. American rights were, by Hale's bad faith, trampled on and practically left without the proud protection that has hitherto always been their boast, and the American flag humiliated and disgraced by Hale's conduct, and his subsequent address to the Viceroy of Egypt, remains unredressed to this day, whilst Italy has already obtained full satisfaction.

I enclose herewith the report of that satisfaction published by the Egyptian press.

A great nation like ours humiliated by the unpardonable bad faith of an officer!—the honor of a comparatively smaller nation triumphantly maintained by a chivalric officer! The citizens and protégés of the great Republic practically without a protector in Egypt!—the rights of the subjects of a smaller power safe in the hands of a worthy agent! No further comment seems to be necessary.

With high respect,

F. DAINESE.

WASHINGTON, *June* 29, 1865.

No. 68.

[Extract from Chronicle of June, 1865]

Redress obtained by Mr. Bruno, Consul General of Italy, from the Viceroy of Egypt, for outrages upon Italian subjects.

Lately the Egyptian police entered an Italian domicil, insulted and bastinadoed a number of Italian subjects; whereupon the Italian consul-general at Alexandria, Mr. Bruno, demanded reparation. We clip the following from the Egyptian newspaper, *Spettator*, which shows the ample satisfaction obtained:

ALEXANDRIA, *May* 24, 1865.

The consul general of Italy has accepted the following as the satisfaction demanded from and granted by the Viceroy of Egypt, who acknowledged the right of the demand:

1. The under-director of the local police, Mustafa Bey, to be dismissed.

2. The Muan (deputy) of police and the chief of brigade also to be dismissed.

3. The chiefs of district and precinct to be dismissed and punished.

4. The guards to suffer severe punishment.

5. The donkey boys to be punished and banished.

6. The minister of police to proceed to the consulate general, and beg the consul's pardon.

7. A superior officer of the Egyptian Government to proceed on board the Italian steamer Etna, and beg the commander's pardon.

8. His Excellency the Governor of Alexandria to proceed officially to the Italian consulate general, and declare the Viceroy's regrets for this unfortunate affair, which painfully afflicted him.

We know also that the Italian consul general will invite the officers of the consulate and those of the sloop-of-war Etna, as well as the representatives of all the corporations of the Italian colony in Egypt, to be present at the solemn execution of this reparation, which will be carried out within a few hours.

While we feel cheered at the friendly solution of so unpleasant an incident, and at his Highness's exhibition of his desire to maintain friendly relations with the Italian Government, nevertheless we cannot abstain from expressing regret that the local authorities should have so long delayed to do right in so important a matter.

HALE'S USURPATION OF JURISDICTION DENOUNCED AND CONDEMNED BY THE COURTS.

Upon L. Papanti's request to Charles Hale to attach Dainese's property and money left with Messrs. Costantinidi Giocci, Verza, and Ralli, merchants, established in Egypt, on the false allegation that said Dainese was indebted in the sum of £1085.18*s*.2*d*, to R. H. Allen & Co., of New York, said Hale *did attach*, and otherwise seize and impede, property valued at over $100,000, without even causing security to be given for damages in case of wrongful detention. One of his decrees, appended to Papanti's request, translated from the Italian, is as follows, viz :

No. 69.

No. 215—Seen the preceding act:

"*We* order the execution of the attachment requested therein of the goods, furniture, money, &c., belonging to Dainese in the hands of Mr. Costantinidi, and that the duplicate and triplicato, together with the present decree, be transmitted to the Royal Greek Consulate for its execution.

(Signed) "CHAS. HALE,
"*Agent and Consul General.*

"ALEXANDRIA, 23*d November*, 1864."

A copy of it was sent by Mr. Costantinidi to Mr. Dainese, who, after vain efforts to check, through the Executive, Hale's usurpation of power, submitted the case to the justices of the Supreme Court of the District of Columbia, from before which the Allens had just dismissed their suit,* to revive it before their more convenient court—that of Charles Hale—and obtained from said justices the following opinion :

No. 70.

Opinion of the Justices of the Supreme Court of the District of Columbia.

The act of Congress entitled "An Act to carry into effect certain provisions in the treaties between the United States and China, and the Ottoman Porte," approved August 11, 1848, and that approved June 22, 1860, confer upon U. S. ministers and consuls, in those and other countries named in said acts, certain jurisdiction, in certain cases: and the 22d section of the former, and 21st section of the latter, of said acts extend that jurisdiction to those functionaries in Turkey. But said jurisdiction, so extended, is only given them for *carrying into effect*, as the purport and language of said acts plainly show, the provisions of said treaties, and is therefore confined to matters named therein.

The treaty with Turkey of May 7, 1830, (8 Stats. at Large, p. 408,) has no provision whatever requiring U. S. ministers or consuls to assume jurisdiction in matters of contract or other controversies between citizens of the United States, resident in the United States, who happen to be temporary sojourners in the dominions of the Porte, which controversies can only be determined by the tribunals of their respective domicils where the contract was made. Therefore no consul of the United States, residing in the Turkish dominions, has any right to assume jurisdiction, try, or determine controversies of a civil character between citizens of the United States domiciled in the United States, and any usurpation of such jurisdiction by any of the consuls in the Turkish dominions, would be regarded in the law as a trespass by the consul thus usurping jurisdiction, for which he would be answerable in damages to the party aggrieved thereby.

WASHINGTON, D. C., *January* 4, 1866.

GEO. P. FISHER,
D. K. CARTTER,
A. B. OLIN.

---

* See records of S. C., D. C., No. 1,414.

DISTRICT OF COLUMBIA, TO WIT:

I, Return J. Meigs, clerk of the Supreme Court of the District of Columbia, do hereby certify that the Hon. David K. Cartter is Chief Justice, and the Hon. George P. Fisher and A. B. Olin, Justices of the Supreme Court of the District of Columbia, and were such at the time of signing the above instrument and writing.

In testimony whereof, I have hereunto subscribed my name and affixed the seal of said court, this 16th day of February, 1866.

[L. S.] R. J. MEIGS, *Clerk.*

DISTRICT OF COLUMBIA, TO WIT:

I, David K. Cartter, Chief Justice of the Supreme Court of the District of Columbia, do hereby certify that the above attestation of Return J. Meigs, clerk of said court, is in due form.

Given under my hand this 16th day of February, 1866.

D. K. CARTTER, *Chief Justice.*

UNITED STATES OF AMERICA, DEPARTMENT OF STATE.

To all to whom these presents shall come, Greeting:

I certify, that David K. Cartter, whose name is subscribed to the paper hereunto annexed, is now, and was at the time of subscribing the same, Chief Justice of the Supreme Court of the District of Columbia, duly commissioned; and that full faith and confidence are due to his acts as such:

In testimony whereof, I, William H. Seward, Secretary of State of the United States, have hereunto subscribed my name and caused the Seal of the Department of State to be affixed.

Done at the City of Washington, this tenth day of August, A. D. 1866, and of the Independence of the United States of America the ninety-first.

[L. S.] WILLIAM H. SEWARD.

Subsequently—last August—Mr. Deputy Marshal Phillips, of this district, undertook to serve upon Mr. Dainese the following two decrees of Charles Hale, with other papers, *summoning (?) Mr. Dainese to proceed to Egypt.*

No. 71.

"CONSULATE-GENERAL OF THE UNITED STATES OF AMERICA
AT ALEXANDRIA, EGYPT.

Richard H. Allen and A. B. Allen vs. *F. Dainese.*

Upon reading the petition of the said Allen in this matter, claiming that the said Dainese is indebted to them in a sum equal to one thousand and eighty-five pounds sterling eighteen shillings and two pence, with interest and costs or less, and the affidavit of Luigi Papanti in support of the same—

It is ordered that an attachment do forthwith issue to attach the several goods, chattels, effects, moneys, and premises of and belonging to the said Dainese; that notice be, and hereby is, given to said Dainese to appear at this consulate-general on Tuesday, the 3d day of January next, at 11 o'clock in the forenoon, at which time and place the cause will be tried according to law.

Witness my hand and the seal of the consulate-general, this 22d day of November, 1864, and of the independence of the United States the 89th.

[SEAL.] (Signed) CHAS. HALE.

CONSULATE GENERAL OF THE UNITED STATES OF AMERICA,
AT ALEXANDRIA, EGYPT, *April* 16, 1866.

In the Matter of R. H. Allen and A. B. Allen vs. *F. Dainese.*

It appears that the said Dainese is now in the United States.

On petition of said Allen—

It is ordered that the said petitioners have leave to procure a copy of the order of this Consulate General of the 22d day of November, in the year one thousand eight hundred and sixty-four, together with a copy of the petition and affidavit therein mentioned, to be served by some disinterested person upon the said Dainese in the United States; and that upon such service, the said Dainese have until Tuesday, the sixteenth day of October next, at eleven o'clock in the forenoon, to appear at this Consulate General, to which time and place the further proceedings herein are hereby adjourned, the previous orders respecting the goods attached meanwhile remaining in force

And it is further ordered, that, unless the said Dainese shall make appearance as aforesaid, at this Consulate General either in person or by duly authorized attorney, on the sixteenth of October, at eleven o'clock, he shall be deemed to be in default, and such proceedings shall thereupon be had therein as if the notice mentioned in said order of twenty-second November had been given to said Dainese personally, within the jurisdiction of this Consulate General.

It is further ordered that a proof copy be served on said Dainese at the same time, and that such service be made on the said Dainese on or before the first day of September, in the year one thousand eight hundred and sixty-six.

In witness whereof, I, Charles Hale, Consul General of the United States of America at Alexandria, Egypt, have hereto set my hand and seal of office, this sixteenth day of April, in the year one thousand eight hundred and sixty-six, and of the Independence of the United States the ninetieth.

[L. S.] (Signed) CHARLES HALE.

No. 72.

CONSULATE GENERAL OF THE UNITED STATES OF AMERICA
AT ALEXANDRIA, EGYPT, *April* 16, 1866.

To Joseph H. Choate, Esq., of the city of New York, United States of America:

You are hereby appointed commissioner, and authorized and empowered to take testimony to be used in an action of the case pending before me, wherein R. H. Allen and A. B. Allen, merchants of the city of New York, are the plaintiffs, and F. Dainese, who is believed now to be within the United States, is the defendant.

You will take no proceedings under this appointment unless it shall be made to appear to you that actual notice thereof has been given to the said defendant by service upon him of a copy of this, my commission, by some disinterested person within the United States.

A copy will be likewise served on the attorney of the plaintiff's within this jurisdiction.

You will put in writing the interrogatories which may be put to witnesses at the instance of either party, with the answers thereto, and return to me such interrogatories and answers on or before the sixteenth day of October next.

In witness whereof, I, Charles Hale, Consul General of the United States of America at Alexandria, Egypt, have hereto set my hand and seal of office this sixteenth day of April, in the year one thousand eight hundred and sixty-six, and of the Independence of the United States the ninetieth.

[L. S.] (Signed) CHARLES HALE.

Upon Mr. Dainese bringing the above illegalities to the notice of the Supreme Court of the State of New York, the following order was entered by that court:

No. 73.

SUPREME COURT.

FRANCIS DAINESE AGAINST RICHARD ALLEN, ANTHONY B. ALLEN, CHARLES HALE, AND JOSEPH H. CHOATE.

On the complaint in this action and the affidavit, of which a copy is hereto annexed.

It is ordered that the defendants in this action show cause before one of the justices of this court at the special term thereof, to be held at chambers at the City Hall of the city of New York, on Monday, the third day of September next, at the opening of the court on that day, or as soon thereafter as counsel can be heard, why the said defendants should not be enjoined and restrained according to the prayer of the plaintiff's complaint; and in the meantime, and until the hearing and decision of this motion—

It is ordered that the said defendants, Richard H. Allen and Anthony B. Allen, their agents, servants, attorneys, and counsellors, desist and refrain from further prosecuting or in any manner proceeding in the suit or action instituted and commenced by them against the plaintiff before the said defendant Hale, at Alexandria, in Egypt, and from authorizing or requesting the said Hale to proceed farther therein; and also that the defendant, Joseph H. Choate, desist and refrain from summoning or examining any witnesses, or acting in any manner under the commission issued to him by said Hale, as alleged in the complaint herein.

GEORGE G. BARNARD,
Justice Supreme Court.

NEW YORK, *August* 31, 1866.

And after hearing the defence of the usurpers, the court entered the additional order hereinafter:

No. 74.

At a special term of the Supreme Court of the State of New York, held at the City Hall, in the City of New York, on the 17*th day of October*, 1866.

Present—Hon. T. W. Clerke, *Justice.*

FRANCIS DAINESE AGAINST RICHARD H. ALLEN, ANTHONY B. ALLEN, CHARLES HALE, AND JOSEPH H. CHOATE.

The motion made by the plaintiff for an injunction coming on to be heard; on reading and filing the plaintiff's complaint and affidavit in support thereof, dated August 28, 1866, and the affidavits of R. H. Allen and Luigi Papanti, on the part of the defendants Allen, and on hearing Samuel J. Glassey and Charles F. Blake, Esqs., of counsel for the plaintiff, and Samuel Newell, Esq., of counsel for the defendants, Richard H. Allen and Anthony B. Allen, it is ordered that until judgment shall be rendered in this action, the said defendants, Richard H. Allen and Anthony B. Allen, be, and they are hereby, restrained and enjoined from further prosecuting or proceeding in any manner, either by themselves, their agents, servants, attorneys, or counsellors, in the action or proceeding instituted by them before the defendant, Charles Hale, at Alexandria, in Egypt, against the plaintiff, or from authorizing or requesting, or directing said Hale to continue to keep possession, or from, in any manner, interfering with the property, credits, and effects of the said plaintiff at Alexandria aforesaid. And it is also ordered that the said defendant, Joseph H. Choate, be, and he is hereby, enjoined and restrained from summoning or examining any witnesses, or acting in any manner under the commission issued to him by said Charles Hale to take testimony in the said proceeding instituted before him by said defendants Allen against said plaintiff.

The defendants Allen to be at liberty to appeal from this order to the general term of this court without security. Ten dollars costs of this motion to abide the event of this action.

WILLIAM C. CONNER, *Clerk.*

[A copy.]

From this order the Hale party appealed to the general term, when the court, after delivering the following opinion, which was adopted *unanimously*, denied Hale's jurisdiction, and made *perpetual* the restriction of proceedings in Egypt.

No. 75.

SUPREME COURT—GENERAL TERM.

DAINESE AGST. ALLEN AND OTHERS.

CLERKE, J.: Even if the judicial authority was vested by the conjoint consent of the government of the United States, and that of the Ottoman Porte, in the American Consul at Alexandria, still it would not be the judicial power contemplated in the third article of the Constitution. The power contemplated by the Constitution is that which is possessed and exercised by regularly organized tribunals, within the territory of the United States; in which actions are prosecuted and justice administered by judges especially appointed according to an established procedure and in a regular and formal manner. The authority given to executive officers to exercise judicial functions, incidentally or occasionally, is not that judicial power to which the third article of the Constitution of the United States has reference; therefore a State court will not refrain from interfering with persons prosecutiug a claim before an American Consul in a foreign country, where the Consul has no jurisdiction of such claim or exercises an authority to which he has no right.

II.

As a general rule, if a party has an adequate remedy at law, a court of equity will not interfere by injunction; but it is sometimes difficult to determine whether he has an adequate remedy, particularly when an injury may be suffered through the instrumentality of judicial proceedings in a foreign country, and therefore as Lord Broughham says, in Canon Iron Co. *vs.* McLarens (5 H. of L., 438,) "if a suit instituted abroad appears ill calculated to answer the ends of justice, the court of chancery will restrain the foreign action."

III.

At the time the proceedings under consideration were commenced before the consul, he had no jurisdiction in civil cases. There are only two treaties, I believe, between the United States and the Ottoman Porte, in which the latter has delegated any portion of judicial authority to the consuls of the former. The treaty of 1830 does, undoubtedly, grant to them in certain cases criminal jurisdiction, but nothing more. The treaty of 1860 has the following provision: "It is moreover expressly stipulated that all rights, privileges and immunities which the Sublime Porte now grants or may hereafter grant to, or suffer to be enjoyed by, the subjects, ships, commerce, or navigation of any other foreign power, shall be equally granted to, exercised, and enjoyed by the citizens, vessels, commerce, and navigation of the United States of America."

It is contended that because the consuls of other nations have exercised jurisdiction in civil cases in Turkey, that this provision delegates the same jurisdiction to American consuls. It does not contain a single word relative to consular authority of any description; it relates solely to privileges allowed to private individuals, and to commerce and to navigation. Before we can decide that a nation parts with any of her sovereign authority, the language by which it is transferred should be direct and unequivocal. From the language quoted it is evident that no such design was ever the subject of negotiation; nor do I think Congress has conferred any such authority upon consuls, although, if it had, the authority would be ineffective without the concurrence of the Ottoman Porte. As we have seen that this concurrence has not been yielded, it is scarcely necessary to examine the acts of Congress relating to this subject with any particularity.

By the act of 1860 judicial power is conferred on consuls in criminal matters, and, in civil cases, with such powers as consuls in China possess, so far as the same is permitted by the laws of Turkey, or its usages in its intercourse with the Franks or other Christian nations. By the treaty with China the jurisdiction of consuls in civil cases is confined to questions between citizens of the United States *residing in China*. Neither party in the proceedings before the consul in Alexandria resided there at the time they were commenced, or at any time since. It is unnecessary to pursue this examination any further, as we have seen that the Ottoman Porte has never yielded any jurisdiction in civil courts to American consuls.

On the whole, I think this injunction ought to be continued. We have jurisdiction over the persons of the defendants; it is a proper case for the exercise of that jurisdiction; and the prosecution of the proceedings before the consul at Alexandria is calculated to be productive of gross injustice.

Order should be affirmed with costs.

[Copy.] O. S. BARBOUR, *Reporter.*

www.ingramcontent.com/pod-product-compliance
Lightning Source LLC
LaVergne TN
LVHW021429110826
845150LV00007B/2156

* 9 7 8 1 4 2 5 5 0 7 2 6 8 *